CONTENTS

QUILTING

AN INTRODUCTION TO AMERICAN PATCHWORK DESIGN

PENNY McMORRIS

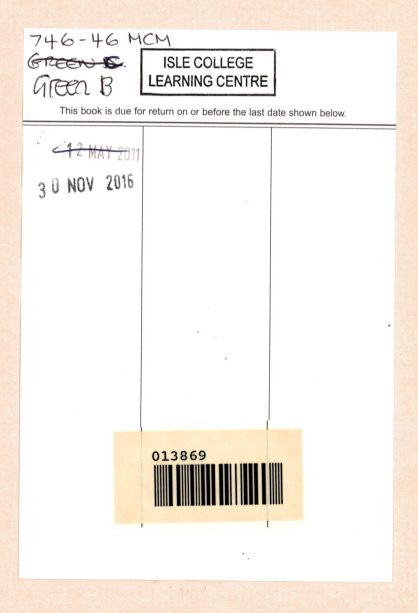
BRITISH BROADCASTING CORPORATION

This book is published in conjunction with the television series
Quilting first transmitted in the UK on BBC TV from Summer 1984
Executive producer: Peter Riding
Book adviser: Deirdre Amsden

Quilted sample on the cover by Jenny Chippindale
of the Royal School of Needlework
Cover photography by Tony Latham
Diagrams by Deborah Bewley

Dedication
For their help I would like to thank Joan Gordon, Jan Bell, Ken
Miller and my director and friend, Paul Lopez
Penny McMorris

First published in 1981 by
WBGU-TV Bowling Green State University
Bowling Green, Ohio 43403, USA
©1981 Television Station WBGU-TV

UK edition with revisions first published in 1984
by the British Broadcasting Corporation
35 Marylebone High Street, London W1M 4AA
©1984 Television Station WBGU-TV

ISBN 0 563 21039 7

Typeset in 11/12 Monophoto Ehrhardt by
August Filmsetting, Haydock, Merseyside
Printed in England by
Chorley & Pickersgill, Crossgates, Leeds
Cover originated and printed by
Belmont Press Limited, Northampton

INTRODUCTION

Many people who admire antique quilts in museums or stately homes never realise that this is a needlework tradition which is still alive today, and that the basic technique is simple enough to be mastered by anyone who can use a needle and thread. Patchwork quilting is an aspect of this craft which is particularly challenging and rewarding. In America it has reached the status of modern folk art and there are now many contemporary artists working in the medium.

This book looks particularly at design in relation to patchwork quilting, but the techniques involved are also clearly explained with much advice on how to produce a finished article which will wash and wear successfully as well as look beautiful. For those interested in the artistic aspect of quilting there are several sections on the work of modern designers, and the quilts featured in the accompanying BBC television series are listed along with details of the quilters who made them. (If patterns are available for any of these, this has been indicated, but bear in mind that most of them are copyright designs.)

You will also find at the end of each chapter a short list of books and magazine articles directly relevant to the topic that has been covered. More comprehensive lists of books, suppliers, museums and quilting societies can be found on pp60–71.

Publisher's note

This book was originally written to supplement the American television series *Quilting*, first shown on BBC Television in Spring 1984. In revising the text for a British audience we have used the English version of certain terms (see below) and have condensed or expanded sections slightly as appropriate. We have also decided to keep to the imperial system of measurements since $\frac{1}{4}$ inch is a convenient and familiar seam allowance used by quilters. (If you prefer to use the metric system, allow 1 cm for your seams.)

All addresses given were correct and all publications available as listed at the time of going to press. The American magazines referred to can be obtained from some specialist shops and are also available on subscription (see p65).

English term	American term
Tack	Baste
Wadding	Batting
Lattice strips	Sashes

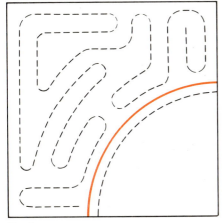
Random

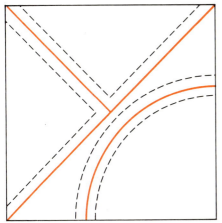
Outline

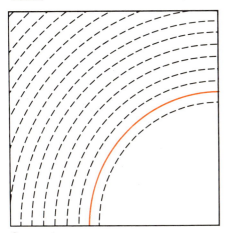
Contour

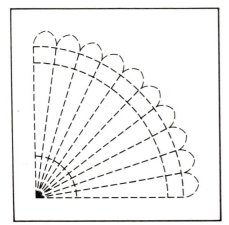
Decorative

The tradition of patchwork quilt-making was born out of a need for warm bed-covers which could be made cheaply from left-over scraps of material. The scraps were pieced together in an attractive design and this 'top' was then attached to a layer of wadding and backing material with rows of small stitches, which made the unstitched areas 'puff out'. Gradually, quilting also developed into a social activity, especially in America where groups of women often gathered to make quilts together, and, as the designs became more intricate, it also became a form of popular art. Quilt-making is still alive today and modern quilters are adding to the traditional designs of the past by developing exciting new design ideas.

Although quilts can be extremely elaborate and intricate, the basic technique is very simple.

The quilting stitch

The most commonly used quilting stitch simply involves taking a running stitch through the three layers to be quilted: top, wadding and backing, which have been tacked together first. One hand guides the needle in and out from the top, while the other hand lies below waiting to feel the needle in order to make sure it is passing through all three layers. With practice you can make your quilting stitches small, straight and evenly spaced.

Although the stitch itself is very simple, producing beautiful quilting designs takes practice and planning. The amount of planning you need to do depends on the type of patterns you want to make. Quilting designs may be divided into four main groups:

Random
Areas of meandering, random stitches. Needs little or no marking. Often used as a background filler, making areas that are not quilted puff out. Sometimes called stippling, it is seen most often in very old quilts where the unquilted areas were sometimes stuffed with additional wadding to make them stand out even further from the densely quilted background.

Outline quilting
Rows of quilting stitches which outline one or both sides of a pieced or appliquéd design. Usually done $\frac{1}{8}$ to $\frac{1}{4}$ inch away from the edge to be outlined. Emphasises individual parts of a pieced design and picks appliquéd designs out from their background fabric. When doing outline quilting, you don't need to mark a line to follow; with practice you can stay an even distance away from the edge you're outlining just by judging with your eye.

Contour quilting
Concentric lines of quilting, often used to outline a pieced or appliquéd design. Sometimes called echo quilting it is most often used in appliqué quilts (eg extensively used in Hawaiian appliqué), but can also be used beautifully in pieced designs and on plain pieces of fabric. Although contour quilting can often be judged by the eye, if you're making rows of straight quilting lines farther apart than $\frac{1}{4}$ inch, you'll find it easier to keep them straight if you mark lines on your quilt top to follow.

Decorative quilting
Quilting designs or pictures which have to be marked on the fabric (although all quilting 'decorates' the fabric surface, giving it texture). This is the type of quilting that most people associate with quilts and one very popular design is the feather wreath (see directions on p11). Border designs also come under this heading and instructions for traditional cable and chain quilting patterns are given on p12.

If you're quilting long, straight lines, you may want to lay strips of masking tape down to mark the line to be quilted. Simply quilt along one or both edges of the tape and then peel off the tape

For more information, see 'Marking Your Quilt' *Quilter's Newsletter Magazine*, March 1980, p8 +

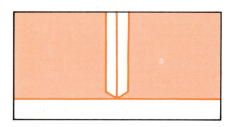

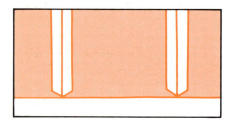

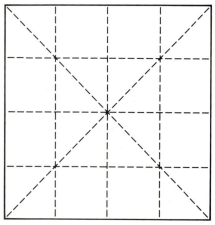

Tacking stitches

Marking

Your designs have to be marked out on the quilt top so that you can then stitch over them. The simplest way to do this to draw around an object or cardboard template straight on to the quilt top with a pencil. You can also use a special fabric marking pen which many craft and sewing shops now stock. The lines made with this will not rub away, as pencil tends to do, while you are stitching. When you have finished quilting, however, you can brush out any lines which show with water and a stiff paint brush. (NB Always test such a pen before you use it to make sure this method actually works on the fabric you have chosen!)

Any design which you can mark on a quilt top can be quilted, so you can try old traditional patterns or invent new ones. Try tracing around household objects such as biscuit cutters, coins, thimbles, or mixing bowls. Use stencils for letters or make tracings of handprints. Make a variety of designs by tracing around the templates used for piecing and appliqué. (You can experiment with designs on paper; try overlapping and turning templates to discover new patterns.) There are also quilting stencils you can buy (see p64). Use them as intended or use parts of them to create original designs.

Marking can be done on the quilt top either before or after it is tacked to the backing and wadding.

Backing

For the back of the quilt use soft *good quality* fabric that is cut 1–2 inches larger than the top on all sides. It should be the same type of fabric as the top so that you can wash the quilt successfully. Don't forget if you are using pure cotton to wash the material first to pre-shrink it, then iron it. If your quilt is to be very wide, you'll need to sew fabric widths together for the back. Either make one or two seams as shown.

Wadding

Many fillings have been, and still are, used to pad the space between quilt top and backing. The two most widely used waddings are cotton and polyester. Cotton wadding gives a flat, traditional look, and needs to be quilted every square inch. Polyester wadding looks puffier than cotton when quilted, and, since it doesn't need to be quilted as closely, it's the best choice for beginners. It is usually sold in 2oz, 4oz and 8oz weights, 2oz being the easiest to sew. When buying polyester wadding, check to see that it has been bonded. An unbonded wadding can work its way up through the quilt top (making the quilt look fuzzy, a condition known as 'bearding'). To check for bonding, take hold of a section of wadding with your hand and tug it. If it comes apart, it isn't bonded.

Tacking

Spread the quilt backing on a large flat surface such as a table or the floor with the right side facing downwards. Spread the wadding (cut to the same size as the backing) over the quilt back. Cover these with your quilt top, face upwards, tugging gently at the backing and wadding to smooth out any wrinkles. You can now tack or pin the three layers together to hold them in place while you are quilting. (The tacks or pins are then removed when the quilt is finished.)

To tack: take large running stitches through all three layers in lines as shown in the diagram (left), starting from the centre and working outwards.

To pin: pin all three layers together, again working from the centre out, placing pins about every 8 inches. (To keep from being pricked as you quilt, use safety pins rather than straight pins.)

Needle and thread

Use any short, not too thick, needle that you're comfortable with. If you're buying new needles, ask for a No 9 Between. Use quilting thread in the colour of your choice. You have several options:

1   You can match your thread to the one colour that is predominant in your quilt.
2   You can change the thread colour every time the fabric colour changes.
3   You can use white or off-white with any colour fabric.
4   You can use a contrasting colour thread.

If you're a beginner you'll find your stitches, which will be uneven at first, will show up less if you match the thread to the fabric.

Quilting thread is becoming more available in Britain. It is stocked by many craft shops (see p61) and the John Lewis chain now sells a limited colour range. Button-hole thread and fine crochet thread are good substitutes, but as they are much thicker, beginners might find them difficult to use. Ordinary cotton thread is not strong enough for quilting.

How to quilt

Once you have tacked your layers together you are ready to begin quilting. If you are making a quilt for a bed you may find the bulk rather difficult to cope with at first. Quilting hoops and frames are available from specialist shops (see p64) and these make life much easier. If you do not have one of these, however, roll up the areas which you are not working on to keep them clean and out of the way.

1   Thread the needle and knot one end.
2   Put the needle into the quilt top about $\frac{1}{2}$ inch away from where you want your first stitch to begin.
3   Draw the needle up where your first stitch is to start. (The needle is to go down *only into the wadding* for this stitch, not through to the backing.)
4   Tug gently to pull the knot down through the quilt top into the wadding. If the knot does not go through, try making the thread hole a little wider by sticking your needle into it and holding it open as you tug the thread. When the knot pops through, it will secure the thread and yet be hidden. (No one should be able to tell where you begin or end a line of quilting; your aim is to give the effect of one endless thread.)
5   Take a running stitch through all three layers of the quilt. (One hand guides the needle; the other hand feels to make sure that every stitch is going through to the back of the quilt.) Take as many stitches as you can comfortably take. Your aim is to make them small, straight and with an even amount of space between each stitch. Some expert quilters take only one stitch at a time. I feel this is a hard way for beginners to learn, however, and think you should learn to do a running stitch first.
6   When you want to end a line of quilting because you have finished an area or run out of thread, you can take a couple of back stitches in a seam of the quilt top where they won't show. If you're not near a seam, carefully take small stitches over the last quilting stitches you've done. In either case, when you take your last stitch, draw the needle through the wadding (but not through the backing) and bring it up about an inch away from where it entered. Clip the thread close to the quilt top and allow the thread to be pulled back into the quilt.

Tie-quilting

Sometimes called 'knotting', this is a quick and simple method of holding your three layers together.

1   Using a strong cotton thread, take a single stitch through all three layers, then a back stitch over it.

Your fingers beneath the quilt will get very sore from needle pricks. Use a bandage to pad your finger so you can still quilt

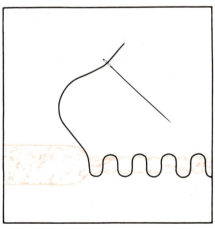

Stitching through three layers

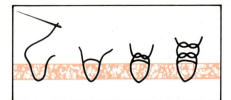

2   Tie the ends of the threads together in a flat or reef knot and trim them.

3   Do this at regular intervals over the quilt, wherever possible on the seams of the patchwork.

The knots can be tied on the back or front of the quilt, depending on your design.

Finishing your quilt

The simplest way to finish off the edges of your quilt is to fold a strip of strong binding round the edge and hand-sew or machine it in place. Do not use bias binding as this will pull out of shape. Do not press the finished quilt either as this will flatten the wadding. If your quilting stitches do not look as good on the back of your quilt as they should do, you can, of course, sew an extra piece of backing material over it!

Quilts in the TV series

BICENTENNIAL FLAG QUILT	Elvena Buchman McCutcheonville Road Pemberville OH 43450, USA
SCHOOLHOUSE TIMES NINE©	Judi Warren 114 E Harrison Street Maumee OH 43537, USA
POINSETTIA MEDALLION©	Fay Goldey 5305 Water Wheel Court Rockville MD 20855, USA
WHAT A RELIEF!© JANUARY 11©	Nancy Crow 10545 Snyder Church Road Baltimore OH 43105, USA
APOTHEOSIS OF EGGPLANT©	Mary Lou Smith 7 Pleasant View Road Wilbraham MA 01095, USA
THISTLE	Nancy Halpern
JACKSTRAWS©	Judy Mathieson 5802 Jumilla Avenue Woodland Hills CA 91367, USA
REDWOOD TREE© STARTING POINT© CRYSTAL ENTRAPMENT©	Katie Pasquini 320 Second Street Eureka CA 95501, USA
SUN, MOON AND STARS©	Margaret Bower 155½ Walnut Avenue Carlsbad CA 92008, USA
SUNTREADER / MONOPHONY©	Michael James

Illustrated in: *Quilt* magazine, Winter 1980

Illustrated in: *Quilter's Newsletter Magazine*, September 1981, p34

Illustrated in: *The Second Quiltmaker's Handbook*, Michael James, p158

Bibliography

Brown, Elsa. *Creative Quilting*
Watson-Guptill Publications, New York, 1975

Colby, Averil. *Quilting*
Batsford Craft Paperback Series, B T Batsford, London, 1983

Dubois, Jean. *The Wool Quilt*
La Plata Press, PO Box 820, Evans, CO 80620, USA
(available by post)

James, Michael. *The Quiltmaker's Handbook*
Prentice-Hall, Inc. Englewood Cliffs, NJ 07632, 1978

James, Michael. *The Second Quiltmaker's Handbook*
Prentice-Hall, Inc. Englewood Cliffs, NJ 07632, 1981

Quilter's Newsletter Magazine, 'Marking Your Quilt', March 1980,
(p8 +)
(available through Craft Publications, Milton Keynes—see p65)

See pp120–126, 24–29, 10–22

See Chapter 5, pp65–88

See Chapter 7, pp136–160

Advantages and disadvantages of various
tools and methods of marking

Feather wreath

The feather wreath is a popular traditional quilting design. Decorative designs such as this one were used to fill in plain blocks in quilts or were placed in areas of special interest in large, otherwise undecorated spaces on quilt tops.

1   Make a tracing of the feather design given here and glue onto a piece of cardboard.
2   Cut round the design to make your feather template.
3   To make a feather rib, use a compass or mark round a circular object such as a mixing bowl. (The size feather given here looks best with a circle that has a diameter of between 9 and 13 inches.)
4   Then mark a slightly smaller circle about $\frac{1}{4}$ inch inside the first.
5   Mark round the feather template inside and outside your circles as shown. Continue this, marking feathers in one direction inside the circle and then reversing them to make mirror images outside the circle. Lay the template each time so that the notch lies on the circle.
6   Fill in the area inside the feather wreath with crossed lines.

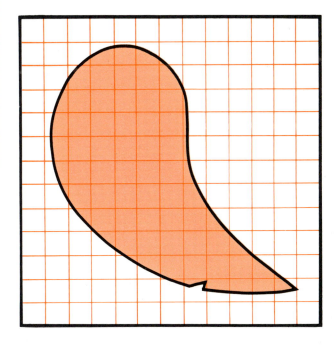

Cable and chain borders

Cable and chain are two traditional designs often used to decorate the borders of a quilt. The template given below can be used for both designs. Trace round it carefully, glue on to card and cut out accurately.

Single chain

1 Place the template on the right side of the fabric to be quilted. Mark round the outer edge, disregarding the two notches.
2 Now move the template to the right until the left-hand point meets the right-hand point marked on the fabric. Mark round the outer edge. Continue until your border is complete.

Single cable

1 Place the template on the right side of your fabric. Mark round the outer edge from the left-hand point over the top to the right-hand notch, then from the left-hand notch underneath to the right-hand point. Also mark completely round the inner hole.
2 Move the template to the right so that the left-hand *outer* point meets the right-hand *inner* point of the marks you have just made. Mark round the template again as just described. Continue until your border is complete.

Obviously, left-handed people will find it easier to start at the right-hand end of their border and move the template to the left every time. Make sure you keep your sequence of markings straight

Chains and cables can be varied by 'doubling' the pattern (see diagrams). For a double chain, mark a second set of outlines over the top of the first set. Begin with the template placed half way between the first two outlines so that the point where they meet is in the centre of the template hole.

For a double cable, mark a line in the centre of your single cable design freehand

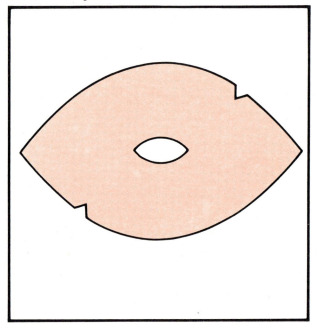

Chain

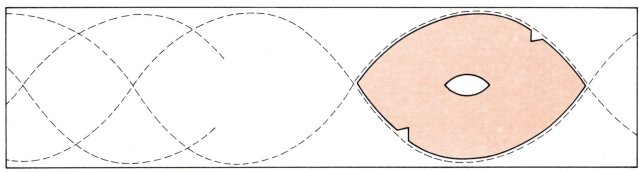

Cable

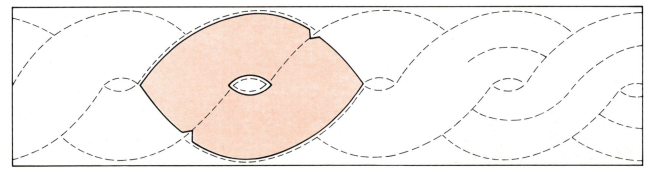

12

2

COLOUR AND DESIGN

English patchwork quilts have traditionally been made either from the centre of the quilt outwards with a large central panel framed by borders, or from one geometric pattern which made up the entire quilt (such as the hexagons used in the design called 'Grandmother's Flower Garden'). American quilt-makers have contributed a new approach to quilt design by using quilt blocks. This involves organising small, usually geometric units like squares, triangles and rectangles into blocks, which are then joined together to make the quilt.

There are hundreds of traditional quilt blocks which can be varied in colour, size and layout to provide an endless number of patterns. You can also devise your own designs for blocks.

Designing quilt blocks

By folding paper

Quilt blocks may be designed by folding squares of paper and letting the fold lines determine the different units of the block.

It's important that you begin with a square that's as perfect as you can make it. Use a set square to help you do this

You can usually find pads of tracing paper in large sheets at art supply shops

1   Start with a square of paper that is the exact size you want your finished patchwork block to be. (Use a thin piece of paper such as tracing or tissue paper.)
2   Fold the square until you get a design of fold lines that you like. Keep unfolding the square as you do this to check the design.
3   To make the design into a quilt block, cut along the fold lines. Paste each separate piece of paper onto cardboard; mark a $\frac{1}{4}$ inch margin all the way round each piece of paper and cut the pieces out round these margin lines. (The reason for this will be explained in the next chapter.)

By using graph paper

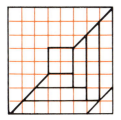

1   Determine how large you want your finished block to be. Then let one square on the graph paper represent 1 inch of your finished block. For example, if you want a finished block 8 inches square, you begin by marking off a block on your graph paper that is eight squares across and eight squares down.
2   Divide up the block by marking lines either along the graph paper lines or diagonally across the graph paper squares. Each separate piece in your graph-paper diagram will be a separate unit of your patchwork block.
3   When you've finished drawing one block, try drawing several blocks together to see how they will look.

When you are happy with your design you can take the measurements directly from the graph paper and make templates in the relevant sizes to use when cutting the fabric for your blocks (see the next chapter).

By cutting paper

1   Cut eight 2-inch paper squares out of each of two or three different-coloured paper sheets. Keep some of these squares whole and cut others diagonally in half and in quarters to make triangles.
2   Paste some of the cut triangles onto squares of a different colour as shown in the diagram (bottom).
3   Make designs by forming a block with a number of paper squares. Try making blocks with four squares, and with nine squares. Turn the paper squares different ways to see how many designs you can form. If you find one that you like, copy it onto graph paper.

Michael James' cut paper exercise

You can obtain more intricate designs by cutting more varied sizes of squares and triangles. Quilt designer Michael James has devised a cut paper exercise which is particularly good for working out new ideas. Begin with four sheets of paper: one black, to represent a dark colour;

13

For a diagram of the lines Michael James marked out, see *The Second Quiltmaker's Handbook*, Michael James, p20

one white, for a light colour; and two shades of grey for in-between colours. After stacking the sheets, mark lines on the top sheet to divide the paper into various sizes of triangles and squares. Then, using a metal ruler and a scalpel, cut through all the sheets of paper at once along all the marked lines. This gives you a large number of squares and triangles to work with when creating your design. When Michael has finished forming a block with paper shapes, he copies the design onto graph paper, shading in the light, dark and in-between values.

Combining blocks

Designs can be changed by the way one block is placed next to another. Rather than seeing individual blocks, you then see the combination of blocks as a whole unit because they merge together visually.

Design *A*, shown left, is symmetrical. No matter which way it is turned it always looks the same. But if you make a block that is asymmetrical, ie different on at least one side, like design *B*, you can produce many different effects by the way you sew your blocks together. Look at the effect produced by sewing four blocks of design *B* together in a particular way *(C)*.

When you find a design that you like, try shading it in a variety of ways and colour combinations to see how many variations you can make.

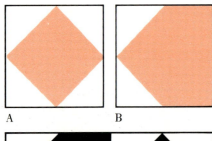

A   B

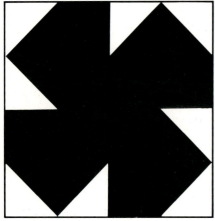

C

Eraser stamp pad

One quick way of seeing how twisting and turning the block will affect your asymmetrical design is by making a rubber stamp out of an eraser and stamping the design on paper, rather than drawing and re-drawing various designs. Here's how to do it:

1 Find a large rubber with a square end.
2 Draw your asymmetrical design, or a simplified version of it, on one square end of the eraser.
3 Cut away the part of the design that is to be light, leaving the part which you want to be dark, using a scalpel or sharp kitchen knife. Cut down about $\frac{1}{8}$ inch.
4 Press the eraser stamp onto a stamp pad and then print your shape on plain paper or graph paper, watching to see how turning the block a quarter turn affects the design.

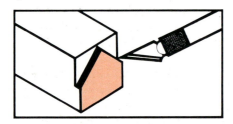

Symmetrical designs

Even though symmetrical designs can't be altered by turning the block, there are other ways to change the overall effect when blocks are combined:

1 Plain blocks can be interspersed with pieced blocks of the same or contrasting colours.
2 Narrow strips of fabric, called lattice strips, can be used to separate the blocks from one another.
3 Setting squares can be added to the lattice strips (see p20 for more information on this aspect of patchwork design).
4 The blocks can be turned so that they are seen as diamonds, rather than squares.
5 The pieced blocks can be combined with other pieced blocks of a different design.

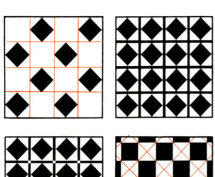

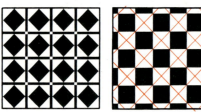

Colour

We've seen how the total look of a design can change according to how quilt blocks are turned and combined with other blocks. Another way in which the design can be changed is by switching the colours and some quilt designs, such as the traditional 'Kaleidoscope', depend on switching the colour of every other block for their effect.

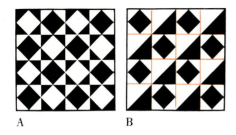

A   B

If you are not familiar with the way in which colours are related to one another, look at a colour wheel in an art shop, or find one illustrated in an encyclopedia

For some good articles on colour, see *Quilter's Newsletter Magazine*, issues 89–94

Look what happens to example *A* when the colours of every second block are reversed.

In example *B*, the block is a relatively simple pieced design in two colours. In a more complicated design, changing the colours used in different blocks within the same quilt can produce even more dramatic differences and emphasise different areas of the same design.

Choosing colour

If you're undecided as to what colours to use in a design, here are some suggestions:

1 Pick one colour (perhaps your favourite) and combine it with white or black. This simple colour scheme works well if you have a particularly strong block design that you want to emphasise.

2 Use lots of different shades of the same colour. You might choose blue, for example, and use printed and plain material in every shade of blue you can find.

3 Try using closely related hues, eg shades of blue plus green and violet.

4 Pick colours that are strong contrasts, eg red and blue, yellow and purple, green and orange.

5 Now try using shades and tints of these strongly contrasting colours (red with light blue, pink and maroon, for example).

6 Use a complete mixture of colours and prints.

Here are some more ideas you may want to use:

1 Let the colours from the wallpaper, paint or furnishings in the room in which you intend to use the quilt suggest some colour combinations to you.

2 Keep an eye out when looking through magazines or visiting art galleries for colour combinations which appeal to you.

3 Cut and paste fabric onto the different units of your graph paper block drawing before you commit yourself to a particular combination. In this way you can get a good idea of what your finished block will look like.

4 Let fabric scraps suggest colour combinations to you. If you keep your scraps together, heaped in a basket, you often notice interesting colour combinations which come together by chance.

5 If you don't have many scraps and cannot obtain samples from local shops, look in quilting magazines for addresses of firms who will send you samples through the post (see also p63).

Designing a quilt involves trying out and discarding a lot of ideas before the final design is reached. This is how Peggy Spaeth, a quilt designer from Ohio in the USA, arrived at designs for two of her quilts:

The design evolved from a simple drawing that I found in a book at a friend's house. (You tend to go around finding patterns everywhere, like a bathroom floor or a book or whatever.) And I found this simple drawing of boxes. I expanded it and drew it, repeating the design so that I had a larger unit. Then I could see what overall pattern was going to happen when the block was expanded. Next I started colouring it in with magic markers in various ways, because I had an idea of how I wanted the design to work, but didn't know which colours, or combinations of colours, were going to make that happen.

I drew it over and over and over again and started colouring it in various ways. Then I found something that worked for me. On the overall pattern, I put all of the red boxes working in one direction and all of the green boxes working in another. I didn't know quite what to do with some of the spaces, so I continued to colour the design in, in different ways. Instead of drawing it over, I just put pieces of tracing graph paper over the grid and coloured it in without drawing it again. You can also photocopy the design and then colour it, as if you had pages and pages of colouring book. I found that the design was

Box Quilt Two-Spaeth

Box Quilt One-Spaeth

starting to work the way I wanted it to work, but I still wasn't happy with some areas, so I experimented more.

What about the borders?

That was the problem. I had both these pieces done and I didn't know how to finish off the borders. I knew that they needed some space around them but I didn't know what kind of space. So I started drawing over and over again these various borders, experimenting with different ways to create space. It's almost like framing a picture. After drawing the whole quilt a few times, I decided to draw it once and then cut out the middle on other pieces of paper so I could draw the border and slip these other sheets over it to try out different arrangements. I went through at least five borders before I decided not to be so elaborate about it, but just to float the design on the lavender that was in the centre. I wasn't happy with such a simple treatment on the other quilt, because I felt it was a stronger design and it had more depth. I think sometimes it takes more time to design a quilt and come up with something worth the effort involved than it does to actually sew the quilt top.

Quilts in the TV series

Notes	Quilt	Quiltmaker
	SCHOOLHOUSE UNTITLED RED	Marjorie Claybrook
Illustrated in *Quilter's Newsletter Magazine*, July/August 1977, p24	KALEIDOSCOPE	Judy Mathieson 5802 Jumilla Avenue Woodland Hills CA 91367, USA
See more of Jan Myers' work in: 'The Presence of Light: The Un-Traditional Quilts of Jan Myers' by Beth Gutcheon, *Fiberarts* magazine, pp60–63 (available from Bayswater Books—see p66)	SPUMONI©	Jan Myers 4234 Longfellow Avenue Minneapolis MN 55407, USA
See: 'Christmas Cactus: From Plant to Quilt' by Michael James, *Quilter's Newsletter Magazine*, November/December 1978, pp16–17	WINTER CACTUS©	Michael James
Picture and pattern given in: *Quilter's Newsletter Magazine*, January 1981, p7	HOMING PIGEON©	Mary Lou Smith 7 Pleasant View Road Wilbraham MA 01095, USA
	FISH TANK TOO©	Diane Avery Weggel 54 Scotland Road Reading MA 01867, USA
Illustrated in: *The Second Quiltmaker's Handbook*, Michael James	RAINY DAY CROCUSES©	Nancy Halpern
Illustrated in: *The Second Quiltmaker's Handbook*	BLUE METAMORPHOSIS© BLACK METAMORPHOSIS©	Francoise Barnes 162 E State Street Athens OH 45701, USA
Illustrated in: *The Second Quiltmaker's Handbook*	NEWE II© NEWE III©	Nancy Crow 10545 Snyder Church Road Baltimore OH 43105, USA
	CHECKMATE© THE ELECTRIC© ELECTRIC II©	Sue Hoyt 380 E Northwood Avenue Columbus OH 43201, USA

Bibliography

Beyer, Jinny. *Patchwork Patterns*
EPM Publications, Inc, 1003 Turkey Run Rd, McLean, VA 22101, 1979; Bell & Hyman, London, 1982

Birren, Faber. *The Textile Colorist*
Van Nostrand Reinhold Co, New York and Wokingham, 1980

Gutcheon, Beth. *The Perfect Patchwork Primer*
David McKay Co, Inc, New York, 1973; Penguin Books, London, 1974

Higgins, Muriel. *New Designs for Machine Patchwork*
Charles Scribner's Sons, New York, 1980; B T Batsford, London, 1980

A good book full of ideas on design and construction whether you sew by machine or not

James, Michael. *The Quiltmaker's Handbook / The Second Quiltmaker's Handbook*
Prentice Hall, Inc, Englewood Cliffs, NJ 07632, 1978/1981

Special sections on design and colour, *The Second Quiltmaker's Handbook*, pp7–53

3

PIECED BLOCK CONSTRUCTION

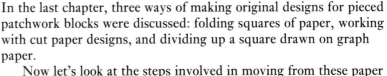

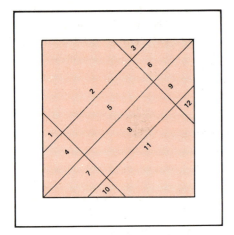

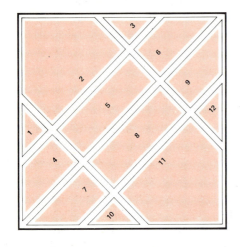

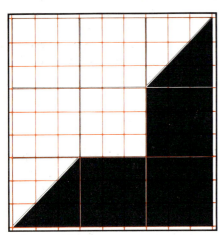

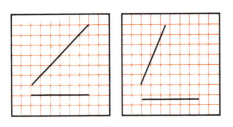

In the last chapter, three ways of making original designs for pieced patchwork blocks were discussed: folding squares of paper, working with cut paper designs, and dividing up a square drawn on graph paper.

Now let's look at the steps involved in moving from these paper designs to finished patchwork blocks:

Folded Paper

Remember that you begin with a square of thin paper the exact size that you want your finished block to be. By folding the paper, you create sections divided by fold lines. Now proceed as follows:

1 Number each section in the design.

2 Make a sketch of the design and fill in the corresponding numbers. (You'll need this sketch to follow, because fitting together the parts of the fabric patchwork block is rather like putting a jigsaw puzzle together.)

3 Divide the folded paper design into sections by cutting along each fold line.

4 Paste each paper section onto cardboard, placing them about 1 inch apart.

5 Mark lines on the cardboard $\frac{1}{4}$ inch away from each paper edge—this is your seam allowance. Cut along this line using scissors, a craft knife or an artist's scalpel (available from art shops).

These will be the templates (patterns) for each piece in your quilt block. (You need a separate template for each piece when using the folded paper method because each piece will be a slightly different size since folding is less accurate than cutting.)

Cut Paper

If your cut paper design is the same size that you want your finished patchwork block to be, you can paste the pieces of cut paper straight onto cardboard, remembering to add $\frac{1}{4}$ inch for the seam allowance, as just described. Then cut the pieces out of the cardboard and use as templates.

If your cut paper designs are smaller than you'd like your finished block to be, you can re-draw the design on graph paper and use this to help you make templates (see below). For example, if you know you have a cut paper design like the one shown left, and you want to make a block exactly 9 inches by 9 inches, you can draw a square which is nine squares across and nine squares down on the graph paper. Then fill in the lines of your design.

Graph Paper

In the last chapter, we were careful to do two things when making the graph paper design: let one square stand for 1 inch in the finished design and stay on the graph paper lines, or move diagonally across the squares from one corner to another. Of course, if you're drawing a design for an entire quilt on a sheet of graph paper, you'll sometimes need to make one graph paper square represent 2, 3 or even 4 inches, in order to fit the whole design on one sheet. However, as long as you stick to the same number of inches per square for the entire design you should have no problems working out measurements for patchwork blocks.

Let's use the traditional Shoo Fly block as an example.

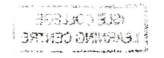

Shoo Fly

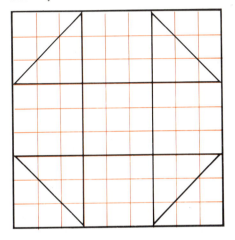

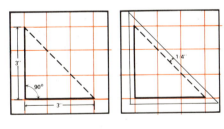

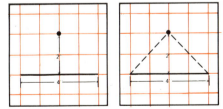

Shoo Fly

1 The Shoo Fly block is a nine-patch block, which simply means that there are nine equal units making up the block, arranged in three rows of three. (Shoo Fly templates are given at the end of this chapter.)

2 Although you could make the block in any size, it is easiest to make it in a size that is a multiple of three. So you could make your finished Shoo Fly block measure 6 inches square (made from nine units that are 2 inches square), or 9 inches square (made from nine units that are 3 inches square), or 12 inches square (made from units 4 inches square), and so on.

3 Draw your design on graph paper. The example shown left uses small units of three squares across and three squares down, to make the entire block nine squares across and nine squares down.

4 You can see that the finished block will have 13 different units in it. But there are only two different shapes in the block: a square and a triangle, which are always the same size. So you will only need to make two templates, one for each of these two shapes.

5 Work out the size of the square by counting the graph paper squares—three squares across and three squares down, making a square that is 3 inches by 3 inches. Draw a square this size on cardboard, using a set square to ensure the corner angles are 90°. Add a $\frac{1}{4}$ inch margin on all sides for seam allowance. Cut out. (Some people like to draw their templates on graph paper, taking advantage of the straight lines and right angles already marked.)

6 Work out the size of the triangle by counting the graph paper squares. In this case, the triangle has two sides that are three squares long, and they meet in a right angle. So draw a line on cardboard that is 3 inches long. At a right angle, draw another line 3 inches long. Connect the ends of these lines with another line. This gives you your triangle. Add $\frac{1}{4}$ inch on all sides for seam allowance and cut out.

The measurements of triangles sometimes seem a little awkward to work out because the lines move diagonally across the graph paper. Always start with what you know. For example, in the diagram shown below left you know that the base of the triangle is a line four squares across. You also know that the peak of the triangle is two squares up from the midpoint of the base line. Draw the base line of 4 inches on cardboard, and then make a point 2 inches up from the middle of the 4 inch line. Draw lines from the peak point to each end of the base line and you have a triangle.

Fabric

Once the templates have been made, you are ready to mark your material. Generally when choosing material you need to think not only how the material will look, but also how it will wear, and how easy it will be to sew and quilt. Normally, light- to medium-weight cottons and cotton mixtures are the best fabrics to use. Do not use any knitted or similar stretchy fabrics. Also avoid heavy fabrics that would be hard to piece and to quilt through. On the other hand, don't use fabrics that are so light and flimsy that they would not wear well. It is best to use the same type of fabric for all your patchwork pieces so that you can wash the finished quilt successfully. Above all, be sure that whatever fabric you use will be worthy of all the time and effort you'll put into making the quilt.

When you've selected your material, pre-shrink it if it is pure cotton, and iron it.

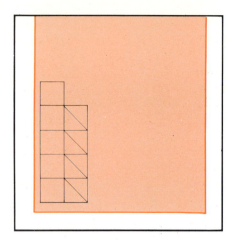

Marking fabric

You can use a variety of things to mark with (I prefer a pencil) but do NOT use ink of any kind, unless it is special marking ink which washes out in cold water.

1   Place the template on the fabric, keeping the main lines parallel to the grain, but don't actually use the selvage as one of your sides.
2   Be aware of any stripes or large patterns in the fabric and plan how you want these to look in your block before you cut it out.
3   Mark on the wrong side of the material. NB If your template is an irregular shape, remember to turn it over before marking round it.
4   Don't leave space between template markings. You've already allowed for seams so you can place your templates right next to one another.

For greatest accuracy, cut each piece separately and cut exactly on your marked lines.

When you have cut your pieces out, you are ready to begin sewing. (If you are making a large pieced-block quilt, sew up a sample block first to see if your marking, cutting and sewing results in a perfect block.)

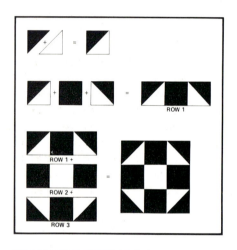

Sewing a block

1   Decide on the order in which the parts of your block are to be sewn. Always try to assemble parts of the block so that they form larger units which can be joined with straight seams.
2   Sew $\frac{1}{4}$ inch seams. (See if your machine measures $\frac{1}{4}$ inch from needle to presser foot outside edge. If not, use a seam guide or strip of tape to mark $\frac{1}{4}$ inch away from the needle. Alternatively, you can measure and mark your seam lines on the wrong side of your patchwork pieces.)
3   When joining two seamed pieces together, first press the seams flat. (If one piece of fabric is light and one dark, press the seam towards the dark side.)
4   Press the finished block.

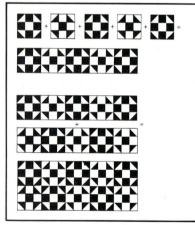

Setting blocks together

Quilt designs can change radically by the way the blocks are set together. Here are some variations on the way in which blocks can be sewn up:

Blocks set directly together
1   Sew blocks into rows.
2   Add one row to another until entire quilt top is sewn. (Carefully match seams by pinning through the seams of both rows before sewing them together.)

Blocks separated by lattice strips
Lattice strips are strips of material which can be used in between patchwork blocks, to make a border for your quilt or even to finish the edges if the material is strong enough. Remember to add $\frac{1}{4}$ inch seam allowance on either side of your strip when cutting out.

1   Sew a block to a lattice strip of the same length; add another block; then a lattice strip, and so on until the row is finished. Sew other blocks and lattice strips into rows.
2   Sew your block/lattice strip row to one long lattice strip. Add the next block/lattice strip row and so on until the quilt top is finished.

Blocks separated by lattice strips with setting squares
1   Sew up your block/lattice strip rows.
2   Now sew a short lattice strip to a setting square (ie a square of material the same width as your strip—see diagram at top of next page); add another short lattice strip, then a setting square, and so on.
3   Sew block/lattice strip rows to lattice strip/setting square rows until quilt top is finished.

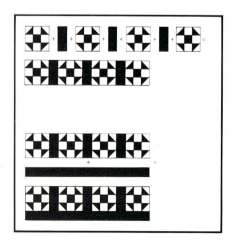

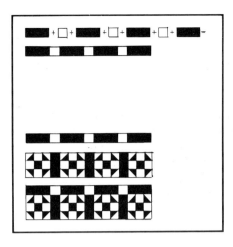

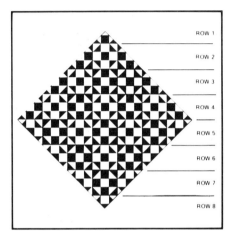

Blocks set as diamonds

1   Setting the blocks on the diagonal means that the blocks on the edges of the quilt will only be half blocks. If plain blocks are being used, you can simply cut pieces from your fabric which are half a normal block cut on the diagonal, plus $\frac{1}{4}$ inch seam allowance on that diagonal cut edge. If pieced blocks are being used, however, you will have to make new templates and make up the required number of triangular blocks.

2   The blocks are then sewn into rows as shown in the diagram. As in all other quilt tops, be careful to match seams.

When you've finished setting your blocks together, press the quilt top and place it on the wadding and backing. Tack or pin (use safety pins) the three layers together and quilt or tie.

There are two factors which determine the beauty of any quilt: workmanship and design. The design of a quilt is extremely important, but poor workmanship will detract considerably from even the most beautiful design. This is what US expert Pat Morris looks for when judging entries in quilt shows in America:

We look at general appearances first of all, the overall effect or the impact. We also, of course, look for workmanship and the size of the quilting stitches. Usually the back is either one or two pieces of fabric. We look to see that the seam is nice and straight and the seam allowance is consistently pressed in the same direction. The colour of thread in the back really doesn't matter. Whatever a quilter wants to use as the quilting thread on top is perfectly all right for the back. All the lines in the quilt should be nice and straight. Many times when people are making a block-to-block quilt and sashing it [setting them with lattice strips], the lines get wobbly and uneven. When you're binding a quilt, if you're going to have a round corner that's fine, take the binding around the corner. If you're going to have a square corner, don't accidentally round it off, which many people are doing. Be precise. It doesn't matter really what method you use, but how well you do that particular method.

Practice blocks

Quilting teachers also stress workmanship as well as design. Judi Warren has taught quilting classes at the Toledo Museum of Art in Ohio, USA for many years and always begins by having her students design and sew a sample block. This is so that her students will gain experience in tracing the templates onto fabric and will also learn to be as accurate as possible. She also wants her students to understand the construction sequence that each block needs. 'Every block goes together in a different way and there's a logical order to joining pieces. Also, there are things like pressing seams and making sure that all the edges that show on the front of the quilt will be sharp, clean, and crisp. In general, a practice block is important so that when units of a block are joined, they go together as smoothly as possible.'

Quilts in the TV series

ART DECO: MAKING Z'S©	Judi Warren
HOT MOBIUS©	114 E Harrison Street
	Maumee
	OH 43537, USA

Art Deco: Making Z's-Warren

Hot Mobius-Warren

Row 1   Row 2   Row 3

Shoo Fly templates

One method of shading (for a 9-inch block)

1   Cut out:
4 dark fabric triangles
4 dark fabric squares
4 light fabric triangles
1 light fabric square
2   Place light and dark triangles together in pairs; then press seams to dark sides.
3   Sew up Rows 1, 2 and 3 as indicated left.
4   Now sew Row 1 to Row 2, matching the seams carefully. Add Row 3 and press finished block.

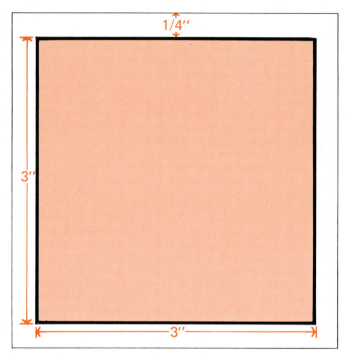

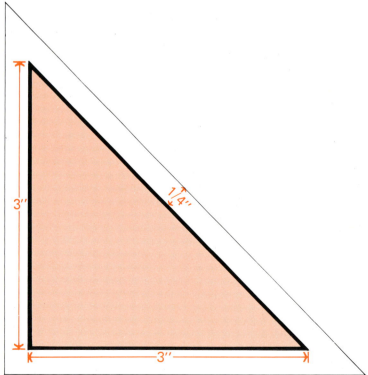

4 LOG CABIN DESIGN

Variations on the basic Log Cabin design can be found in quilts from the turn of the century where the influence of the crazy quilt (see p49) is reflected in the use of rich embroidery and fragmented strips

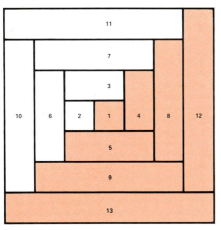

Log Cabin block

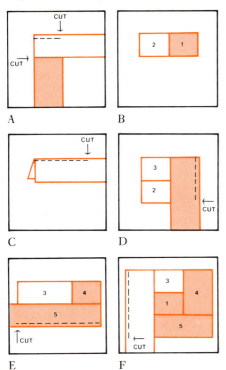

A   B

C   D

E   F

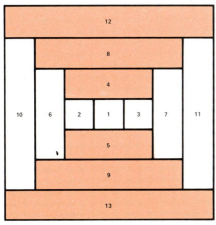

Courthouse Steps

The Log Cabin design is an old traditional pattern. Over the years, the fabrics used in these quilts have changed from wools to velvets and cottons, but the basic block design has remained more or less the same. The traditional block is a simple one, but it can be combined with similar blocks in a variety of ways to form a large number of designs.

How to make a Log Cabin block

The Log Cabin block is one of the few blocks which does not need a template at all. Begin by marking out equal numbers of long strips on the wrong side of two different shades of fabric, one light and one dark. The strips can be any width you like but it is best to start off with ones that aren't too narrow, say 1 inch. Use a yardstick or long ruler and pencil to mark your strips, being careful to keep them parallel with the grain of the material. Cut the strips out, being careful to add $\frac{1}{4}$ inch on each side for your seams, and keep the two types separate. (You can, of course, use more than two fabrics but it is traditional to have half the strips light shades of a colour and half dark shades of the same or a toning colour.)

1   Take one light strip and one dark strip and pin them, right sides together, at right angles (see diagram *A*) along the seam line marked on the light strip. Sew across the width of the dark strip, then cut away the strips as indicated. Open up your two 'logs' and press the seam to one side.

2   Now take another light strip and pin it on top of the first two logs, right sides together. Sew along the marked seam line at the top (*C*), then cut off the strip where it extends beyond the other logs.

3   Open out the new log (no 3), press the seam to one side, then place a *dark* strip on top of the sewn logs, down the *right hand side* (*D*). Sew along the seam line marked on the right and cut away the overlapping strip.

4   Open out the new log (no 4) and place a dark strip (again) along the *bottom* of the sewn logs (*E*). Sew along the marked seam line at the bottom, cut off the overlapping strip and open out the new log.

5   Now take a light strip, place it on the sewn logs on the *left-hand side* of the group (*F*). Sew along the seam line marked on the left, cut away the overlap and open out the new log.

You have now worked right the way round your block of logs once. Continue this procedure until you have a block the size you require. Make sure you always follow these rules:

●   Sew two light strips, then two dark, then two light etc.
●   Work in a clockwise direction, keeping the new strip on top and the sewn logs underneath.
●   If you have to put the block down before you have finished it, remember that the last log added is always the one that runs the *entire* width of the unfinished block.

Courthouse Steps variation

One variation of the traditional Log Cabin block is called Courthouse Steps and can be sewn by the method just described. In this design, each colour usually repeats in the strip directly opposite it, making a block that is divided in quarters rather than halves.

    The strips are sewn in a slightly different order. Begin with your two centre logs as described above. The next unit is then added on the *opposite* side to log no 2, and cut so that it is the same size as the other two (so that you have, in effect, three squares). The next unit (using the second colour strip) is then added, and a corresponding one opposite, and so on (in the order numbered) until the block is finished.

23

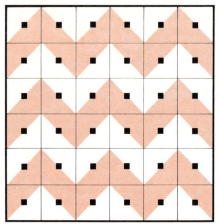

Zig Zag

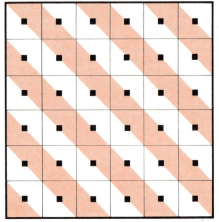

Straight Furrow

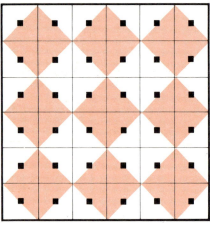

Sunshine and Shadow

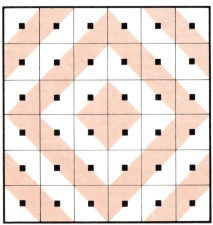

Barn Raising

Form designs by combining blocks

One large block could be used for the front of a cushion cover as could, say, four smaller blocks. (If you're covering a rectangular cushion, just extend the sides of the block out with extra 'logs' until it is the correct size.) Log Cabins are traditionally quilted along one or both sides of each log. Whenever you use more than one Log Cabin block you get into some interesting design possibilities. Since the block is divided into lights and darks (called a 'split block'), each time the block is turned a quarter turn, in relation to the other blocks, a different design is formed. With four blocks you can get a few design variations; with more blocks the design possibilities seem endless. Quilt-makers usually find these designs by laying out all their finished blocks on a flat surface and turning them one way and another until they find a design that they like. Some of these designs have become very well-known and have been given descriptive names.

The 'Zig Zag', for example (sometimes called 'Streaks of Lightning'), has jagged stripes of light and dark which move down or across the quilt. Long stripes that run diagonally across the quilt are known as 'Straight Furrow', and when the quilt blocks are arranged so that groups of four blocks meet with their dark halves touching, the resulting design is known as 'Sunshine and Shadow' because of the alternating light and dark diamonds. One of these diamonds forms the centre of what is possibly the best-known and most popular variation, 'Barn Raising'. The strips which surround the central diamond supposedly resemble the sides of a newly built barn before they have been raised into place.

These strong Log Cabin designs are greatly admired by quilt collectors and dealers. Darwin Bearley, a US quilt dealer, has a small but rare collection of Amish Log Cabin quilts (see p45) and has studied their history:

How have the fabrics used in Log Cabin quilts changed?
Quite a few were made in the last half of the 19th century, and in most of these, the women used a fine wool serge, or mohair, or wool challis—a very fine soft wool fabric. They also used a lot of silks and satins most commonly seen in Victorian crazy quilts but also in quite a few Log Cabin quilts as well. In the 20th century, quilt-makers started becoming more interested in cotton fabric. There were more cotton mills producing at that time, so, of course, there was more cotton available. Fabrics like cotton sateen were also used, especially in Midwest Amish quilts.

As the material changed, did the design change?
There are quite a few variations possible because of the nature of the individual blocks and the positioning of the lighter and darker fabrics. The quilt pattern is basically a very simple one, and it was just up to the individual quilt-maker's imagination as to what she could do with that individual block in putting together different combinations to get different designs. Then, of course, there were little changes too. For instance, one quilt has the centre, or what people refer to as the chimney, of the Log Cabin block divided in half diagonally, which adds a nice kind of change in the overall pattern.

Is Log Cabin still a popular pattern today?
Yes, I think most people who get into quilt collecting always seem to want an example of a Log Cabin quilt.

Quilts in the TV series

Pattern available by post from Judy Mathieson. Also see: 'Judy's Coats' by Bruna Jones, in *Quilt* magazine, Summer 1980	LOG CABIN JACKET©	Judy Mathieson 5802 Jumilla Avenue Woodland Hills CA 91367, USA
	LOG CABIN (*with family photographs*)	Mary Lou Ridley R No 2, Box 249 South Haven MI 49090, USA
Illustrated in: *Log Cabin Quilts*, Leman and Martin, p16	SEASCAPE©	Flavin Glover 744 Briarwood Avenue Auburn AL 36830, USA
Illustrated in: *Fiberarts* magazine, September/October 1979	FENCES©	Virginia Randles 6 Strouds Run Athens OH 45701, USA
Illustrated in: *Quilt* magazine, Autumn 1980, p16, and *The Second Quiltmaker's Handbook*, Michael James	LOG CABIN VARIATION©	Maria McCormick-Snyder 9 Albany Street Cazenovia NY 13035, USA
Illustrated in: *Quilt* magazine, Autumn 1980, p16	ART DECO©	
Illustrated in: *Quilter's Newsletter Magazine*, January 1981, p2	CHRYSALIS©	

Bibliography

Cox, Patricia. *The Log Cabin Workbook*
One of a Kind Quilting Designs, 6601 Normandale Rd, Minneapolis, MN 55435, USA, 1980 (available by post)

James, Michael. *The Second Quiltmaker's Handbook*
Prentice-Hall, Inc, Englewood Cliffs, NJ 07632, 1981

Leman, Bonnie, 'Easy Log Cabin: Machine Piecing'
Quilter's Newsletter Magazine, April 1977, p29

McMorris, Penny. *Crazy Quilts*
E P Dutton, New York, 1984

Leman, Bonnie, and Martin, Judy. *Log Cabin Quilts*
Moon over the Mountain Publishing Co, 6700 W 44 Ave, Wheatridge, CO 80033, USA, 1980 (available by post)

Saffell, Mildred D. 'Easy Log Cabin: Handpiecing'
Quilter's Newsletter Magazine, April 1977, p29

Wien, Carol. *The Great American Log Cabin Quilt Book*
E P Dutton, New York, 1981 (new edition)

For suggestions on innovative Log Cabin design, see pp106–135

Gives many Log Cabin variations and charts to help you work out the exact yardage of strips you will require

5

STRIP QUILTS

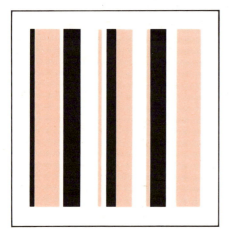

Strip design

Lightning Stripes

Flying Geese

Tree Everlasting

Seminole Patchwork

For a detailed description of this method, see: *The Second Quiltmaker's Handbook*, Michael James, pp87–105

The strip quilt is an early quilt design which originated in England and Ireland. At its simplest, it is just strips of fabric sewn together which run the whole length or width of the quilt. If you'd like to try a simple strip quilt, draw a combination of stripes of the same or different widths on graph paper, playing around with different colours and border designs. When you find a design that you like, let the graph paper squares tell you how long and wide to cut the strips. After sewing up the strips to make your quilt top, you might like to quilt along them, using quilting designs usually used on borders. This would include many different cable and chain designs (see p12).

Your strips can also be pieced together from smaller units. One traditional strip design made of rows of triangles pieced together is called the 'Zig Zag' or 'Lightning Stripes'. The triangles should have equal base to height, and half-triangles are needed at either end of each strip. The strips are then joined together to form the quilt top. Notice how the colours of the triangles are arranged in the example given here. It is the careful arrangement of lights and darks that produces the zig zag effect.

Another traditional strip design is 'Flying Geese'. Here dark triangles are sewn, with two light half-triangles either side, into strips. The strips are then sewn together with the triangles pointing alternate ways so that they give the impression of geese in flight.

The design called 'Tree Everlasting' is made with long plain strips of light and dark combined with strips pieced from triangles.

All of these are strip quilts since they are joined together in strips rather than in blocks.

Strips can also be used in another way. By sewing strips together and then cutting the combined strips and re-sewing them in a different way, you can create unique patterns. This sewing/cutting/re-sewing process is the basis of a method known as Seminole patchwork.

Seminole patchwork

Seminole patchwork is the name given to the elaborate strip piecing method developed by Seminole Indian women in the USA about 60 years ago and is still done by them today. The basic steps used in simple Seminole designs are as follows:

1   Various strips of fabric are sewn together.
2   These combined strips are then cut up (allowing $\frac{1}{4}$ inch for seams) either by cutting straight across the strips or by cutting diagonally.
3   The cut pieces are then re-arranged and re-sewn.

The easiest way to practise Seminole patchwork methods without wasting material is by working with strips of paper. Cut up strips of coloured paper, tape them together, then cut and re-tape them to see how different Seminole strip designs are formed. Don't forget when you come to try a design out using fabric strips, however, that you must allow for seams of $\frac{1}{4}$ inch on all sides.

Since Seminole patchwork is done in strips, you can use several strips to make border designs or combine rows of Seminole strips with plain strips to make cushion or quilt tops. Traditional Seminole patchwork was done using plain coloured fabric—often red, yellow, black and white—but you can create different effects by using stripes and prints as well.

Contemporary American quilt designers like Michael James and Nancy Crow are using ideas derived from Seminole techniques. They make exciting and complex designs by sewing strips of fabric together and then marking this new yardage of material with templates, cutting it and re-sewing it (sometimes several times) to make the final quilt.

With two strips

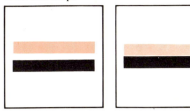

With three strips

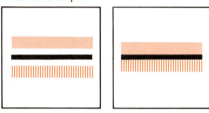

With five strips

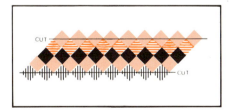

Here are three different designs using strip piecing methods which may give you ideas for improvising your own.

With two strips

1 Begin with two strips of equal width.
2 Sew the strips together, using $\frac{1}{4}$ inch seams.
3 Cut the strip into segments of equal width.
4 Sew these segments together again, but reverse the colour order of every other segment.

With three strips

1 Begin with three strips—two of equal width and one narrower than the other two.
2 Sew the strips together with the narrower strip in the middle.
3 Cut the strip into segments of equal width, cutting diagonally across the strip.
4 Sew the segments together as shown in the diagram, forming a strip of diagonal stripes. Then cut the points off the top and bottom of the band to form a long strip with straight edges.

With five strips

1 Begin with five strips of equal width.
2 Sew the strips together.
3 Cut straight down the strip to form segments of equal width.
4 Sew the segments together as shown in the diagram, lining up the colours so that one colour is joined directly to the colour above it on the next strip.
5 Cut the points off the top and bottom of the band so that you have straight edges to your final strip.

Seminole patchwork vest-Weggel

Quilts in the TV series

AURORA AUSTRALIS©	Sue Hoyt 380 E Northwood Avenue Columbus OH 43201, USA
HILL TEMPLE©	Jan Myers 4234 Longfellow Avenue Minneapolis MN 55407, USA
SPECTRUM BARS©	Virginia Randles 6 Strouds Run Athens OH 45701, USA
FLYING GEESE BABY QUILT	Terrie Mangat 3 Madison Lane Cincinnati OH 45208, USA
RED MAPLE'S YEAR©	Nancy Halpern
SEMINOLE-STYLE PATCHWORK PILLOWS©	Michael James
SEMINOLE PATCHWORK VEST©	Diane Avery Weggel 54 Scotland Road Reading MA 01867, USA
NEWE II©	Nancy Crow 10545 Snyder Church Road Baltimore OH 43105, USA
SUNDOWN©	Virginia Randles
NIGHT PIECE© PAVEMENT OF HAPPINESS© DIALOGUE© DELIVERANCE©	Radka Donnell

For more on Radka Donnell, see: *Fiberarts* magazine, September/October 1979, p81; September/October 1980, pp 76–77

Bibliography

Bradkin, Cheryl. *The Seminole Patchwork Book*
Yours Truly, Inc, 1980 (available here in some specialist shops)

Dudley, Taimi. *Strip Patchwork*
Van Nostrand Reinhold Co, New York and Wokingham, 1980

Garoutte, Sally. 'Seminole Patchwork' *Quilter's Newsletter Magazine*, October 1974, pp 11–12

'Seminole Patchwork' *Quilter's Newsletter Magazine*, July/August 1980, pp 8–10

Wittmann, Lassie. *Seminole Patchwork Patterns*
2221 76th Ave, Bellevue, WA 98004, USA, 1979 (available by post)

For information about the Seminole Indians see:

National Geographic, December, 1956, pp819–40
National Geographic, November, 1969, pp716–34

6

Friendship Star

Ohio Star

A good source of star block designs is the *Illustrated Index to Traditional Quilt Patterns*, Mills, p1-28

Try using rubber cement for gluing paper templates to cardboard. Any excess glue that oozes out can then be allowed to dry and be easily rubbed off

The star motif

The star is one of the most popular motifs used in pieced quilts and is found in hundreds of different patterns. Long before the star was used in quilting, of course, the symbol appeared constantly in the art of both eastern and western civilisations. It was used to indicate the presence of divinity and spiritual wisdom, and to signify eternal life. The star also symbolised fertility and good luck and in the USA was often painted on barns as it was thought to protect them from witchcraft and lightning.

The star motif is particularly popular in America and some of the earliest American quilts were pieced with designs based on stars. The names given to these star patterns suggest that some of the early symbolism of the star was carried over into its use in quilting—names like 'Star of Bethlehem', 'Christmas Star' and 'King David's Crown'.

Other US star designs have a political significance. The 'Lemoyne Star', for example, was named for the Lemoyne brothers who founded the City of New Orleans in 1718. Many were named after states, carrying the symbolic use of stars on flags over into quilt design. The 'Ohio Star', 'Texas Star', 'California Star', 'Virginia Star' and the 'Star of North Carolina' are a few examples. Sometimes blocks were created to celebrate a territory officially becoming a state. Other stars such as the 'Dolly Madison Star' and the 'Martha Washington Star' were named after popular figures. Star designs were also inspired by nature and were given names like 'Spider Web Star', 'Flying Swallows', 'Falling Star' and the 'North Star'.

The 'Shoo Fly' block (shown in Chapter 3) can be altered to make an easy star block—the 'Friendship Star'. The 'Friendship Star' uses the same 13 pieces as the 'Shoo Fly' but they are arranged in a different way (see diagram).

You can make another star simply by changing the triangles used in the 'Friendship Star'. Rather than making a square by sewing two triangles together (as in the middle square in the top row of the 'Friendship Star'), use four triangles to make up your square. This makes the 'Ohio Star', an example of an 8-pointed star.

Directions for making an Ohio Star block

Templates needed for a 9-inch block

● One square 3 inches by 3 inches plus added seam allowance of $\frac{1}{4}$ inch on all sides.
● One triangle 3 inches at base and $1\frac{1}{2}$ inches from centre of base to peak of triangle. Add $\frac{1}{4}$ inch seam allowance on all sides.

Either make your own or trace round the templates on p32, glue onto thin cardboard and cut out.

Marking and cutting
1 Select fabric in two different colours or prints.
2 Place the templates on the straight of the material and trace around them with a pencil.
3 From fabric *A* cut one square and eight triangles; from fabric *B* cut four squares and eight triangles.

Sewing
1 Sew pairs of triangles of fabric A and B together, using $\frac{1}{4}$ inch for the seam, joining along the short sides of the triangles. Press seams to side.
2 Sew pairs of joined triangles together to form a square as shown. Be careful to match up seams where the triangles meet. Press flat.
3 Sew plain squares to pieced squares to make three rows as shown. Be careful to have the light and dark triangles pointing in the

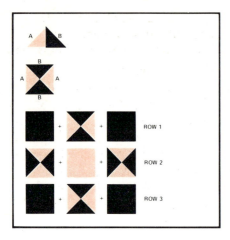

For a good method of sewing diamonds together by machine, see: *The Lone Star Quilt Handbook*, Young and Young

Virginia Star

Rainbow Star—Pulford collection

Indian Heads—Pulford collection

directions shown here so that they will make the points in your star. Press seams flat.

4 Sew Row 1 to Row 2, then add Row 3. Press finished block.

This is only one simple way to make an 'Ohio Star' using two colours or prints. Experiment with different ways of using colour in your blocks to discover ways of varying this basic design.

Stars made with diamonds

So far we've been working with stars based on squares and triangles, but there are many other designs which are based on diamonds. In the 'Virginia Star' (shown left) every point of the star is made from four diamonds. Stars pieced with diamonds can be sewn by machine, but as they require careful adjustments while they're being sewn, it is probably safer to sew them by hand.

Morning Star quilts

Some of the most interesting contemporary quilt designs featuring stars pieced from diamonds can be found on quilts made by the American Indians of the Northern Plains tribes. The star design is especially popular with these Indians as for them it symbolises the morning star and the beginning of a new day. After being introduced to the art of quilting by early American settlers, the Plains Indian women developed designs based on the colours and geometric patterning used in their painting, beading and quill work. Quilts have now become an integral part of the Plains Indians' cultural tradition and are often given as gifts to commemorate such occasions as births, weddings or the award of special honours. The quilts are not normally made for sale, however, so few people are familiar with this Indian art.

One person who *is* very familiar with them is Florence Pulford, from Los Altos, California. Her friendship with Indian families living on reservations in Montana and North and South Dakota, and admiration of their quilting skills led her, after many years, to persuade a number of them to make quilts to exhibit and sell. She now travels and lectures on their behalf and returns profits from the sale of quilts to the Indians. Here she answers some questions put to her about Indian quilts, of which she has a large collection.

How do the Indians use the morning star as a symbol?
In the very beginning of the tribal villages, the camp criers would ride through the villages in the morning calling, 'Awake. Come see the morning star'. And so the morning star is the beginning of a new day. It also is a manifestation of everything that they believe in. It's part of the heavens. So consequently, this is their favourite theme. And they develop all their sub-themes of weather, rainbows, storms and their own personal feelings in the shape of a star.

Does the quilting in concentric rings which they often use stand for something?
Well, many of the women call them the clouds. It gives a very soft feeling to the quilts, and I think for most of them, that's their favourite way of quilting.

These quilts are mainly kept for their own use and are not for sale, is that right?
That's true. Many people save a special quilt to be wrapped in when they die. Other people are given a quilt as a celebration of some honour. Or a woman will give quilts if her son returns safely from the armed forces. If a family I know has someone who dies, I send them a quilt in sympathy.

Do you see any relationship between the geometric patterns they use and their earlier quill and bead work?
Yes, their first quill work, their painting, their bead work frequently used the star, so they feel that the star was not introduced to them. It's a part of their culture and their tradition of watching the universe as

long as there have been Indian people. Also, I think they're truly colour artists. This is one of the things that struck me first—the incredible use of colour. It showed adventure; it showed no holds were barred. I have learned that anything goes in the use of colour.

Can you tell us something about the individuals who make the quilts?
Well, I think I'd like to talk about Almira Buffalo Bow Jackson, who is an Assiniboi. Almira, I feel, is a truly magnificent artist. She makes a different scene in a star for every quilt that she does. And then she has little sub-themes of colour. She used one that had very dark blue in it. And she said, 'This dark blue says, "Sometime I will die". But this red that goes through this part says, "But I am still going to live for a while".' So you see, everything they're talking about in colour is about their life.

Quilts in the TV series

STAR OF BETHLEHEM	Elvena Buchman McCutcheonville Road Pemberville OH 43450, USA
STAR SAMPLER QUILT©	June Ryker 1464 South Ward Street Lakewood CO 80228, USA
CHRISTMAS STAR SAMPLER©	Mary K Richmond 15410 Yukon Avenue Lawndale CA 90260, USA
CALIFORNIA MEDALLION©	Judy Mathieson 5802 Jumilla Avenue Woodland Hills CA 91367, USA
SHADRACH'S COAT©	Sue Hoyt 380 E Northwood Avenue Columbus OH 43201, USA
BOXES AND STARS©	Peggy Spaeth 1672 Eddington Cleveland Heights OH 44118, USA
FLYING CARPET©	Nancy Halpern
COSMIC KALEIDOSCOPE©	Katie Pasquini 320 Second Street Suite 1C Eureka CA 95501, USA
EYES OF ISIS©	Francoise Barnes 162 E State Street Athens OH 45701, USA
BITTERSWEET IV©	Nancy Crow 10545 Snyder Church Road Baltimore OH 43105, USA

For information on other Indian quilt-makers, see: 'American Indian Quilts' by Kenneth Canfield, *Quilter's Newsletter Magazine*, June 1976, pp16–17

Patterns for star blocks used in this quilt available from June Ryker; quilt illustrated in *Quilter's Newsletter Magazine*, July/August 1977, p14

Illustrated in: *Quilter's Newsletter Magazine*, November/December 1980, p29 (includes patterns for two of the blocks)

Illustrated in: *Quilter's Newsletter Magazine*, February 1979, p20 (includes pattern for 'California Star' block used in centre of quilt)

Illustrated in: *The Second Quiltmaker's Handbook*, Michael James

Illustrated in: *Quilter's Newsletter Magazine*, February 1981, p2

Illustrated in: *The Second Quiltmaker's Handbook*, Michael James

Star Sampler—Ryker

Ohio Star

Bibliography

DuBois, Jean. *A Galaxy of Stars: America's Favorite Quilts*
La Plata Press, PO Box 820, Evans, CO 80620, USA, 1976
(available by post)

Mills, Susan Winter. *Illustrated Index to Traditional Quilt Patterns*
Arco Publishing Inc, 219 Park Ave, New York, NY 10003, 1980

Young, Blanche, and Young, Helen. *The Lone Star Quilt Handbook*
Young Publications, Box 925, Oakview, CA 93022, USA, 1979
(available here in some specialist shops)

Ohio Star

Directions:

1   Trace round template patterns given below, then paste tracing sheet onto cardboard.
2   Cut out along outer line.
3   Place templates on fabric and trace around them with pencil.
4   Cut and sew as described on p29.

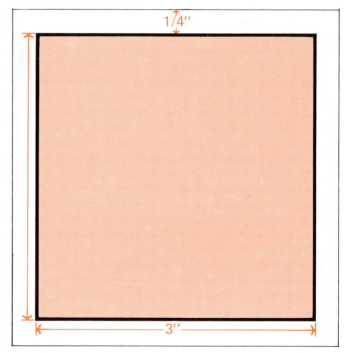

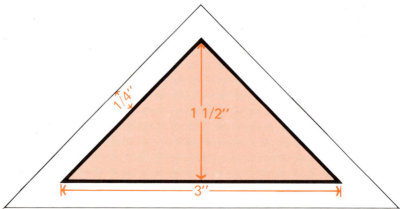

The technique of appliqué involves sewing small pieces of material on top of a larger background fabric by turning all the raw edges under and securing them in place with small stitches. Since any design that can be cut out can be appliquéd, appliqué quilts tend to be more free and curvilinear in design than pieced quilts. Appliqué can also be used for more naturalistic designs than piecing; pieced blocks are usually forced to be abstract because they are made up primarily of straight lines.

Some quilt patterns combine piecing and appliqué. Pieced baskets are often topped with appliqué handles, for example, and many pieced flower designs have appliquéd leaves and stems. Another way in which piecing and appliqué are sometimes combined is in designs like the 'Dresden Plate' (not illustrated), in which the plate is pieced and then appliquéd onto the background fabric.

Symmetrical designs

Just as with pieced blocks, appliqué designs can be divided into symmetrical and asymmetrical patterns. The 'Ohio Rose' is an example of a symmetrical appliqué design—whether you fold it in half vertically, horizontally or diagonally the two halves are exactly the same as each other. This design begins at the centre and radiates out. Symmetrical designs like this are easy to cut from folded paper.

Cutting appliqué designs from folded paper

One fold

Fold a sheet of paper in half. Then cut out any shape freehand, beginning and ending on the fold. You will end up with a shape that is made up of two equal halves joined in the centre. (This is the same principle as that used to cut out chains of paper dolls.) Some suitable shapes to cut out using only one fold are leaves, petals and sprigs of flowers on stems, among other things.

Two folds

Fold the paper in half and then fold in half again. Cut across all the thicknesses of paper from one folded side to the other using straight or curved lines. When you open out your design you will have a shape that is divided into four equal sections, so this is a good method of obtaining circular or oval shapes, and also flowers. Or cut irregular shapes like the one shown in the diagram.

Three folds

Fold paper as described for two folds, then fold again along the diagonal (as if you were making a paper snowflake). Cut a shape from fold to fold again as described above.

Paper is less expensive than fabric, so spend some time experimenting by folding and cutting out shapes of all kinds. When you have cut a number of different shapes, lay them out on a table and try out combinations of shapes on top of or alongside one another. Many of the most intricate and beautiful appliqué patterns are formed by combining symmetrical designs in this way. Experiment and create some original designs of your own.

Asymmetrical designs

For asymmetrical designs (any design that can't be divided into equal parts), you can draw, trace, or cut freehand. Nearly any design that you can draw can be made into an appliqué. Alternatively, you can trace a design from a book or another quilt.

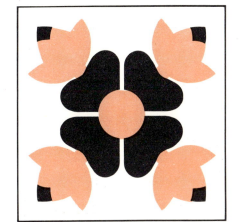

Ohio Rose

One fold

Two folds

Three folds

Making templates

1 Make a design by cutting folded paper or by drawing or tracing a shape onto paper. Your design should be the size you want your finished appliqué to be—don't add a seam allowance.
2 Paste the design onto cardboard and cut out.

Marking and cutting fabric

1 Place the template on the right side of your fabric. Trace round the design with a pencil.
2 Cut out the appliqué, NOT along the pencil lines, but $\frac{1}{4}$ inch outside the pencil lines. This extra $\frac{1}{4}$ inch will be folded underneath when you sew the appliqué onto your background fabric. The pencil line you have drawn will act as a guide to show you where to fold the raw edge under.

As you get more confident, you can, of course, mark shapes freehand onto your fabric and cut them out (allowing $\frac{1}{4}$ inch for folding under).

Sewing on the appliqué

Let's use a traditional pattern for a boy in overalls as an example. (Templates for a boy and girl are given on pages 37 and 38.)

1 Trace round the templates provided, then paste onto cardboard and cut out as described above.
2 Mark and cut your fabric as described above. Be careful to mark the templates on the straight grain of the material.
3 Place the overalls over the shirt, tuck the tops of the shoes under the overall legs and place the hat on top of the shoulder area. As you do this, notice which raw edges will be covered by other pieces and which raw edges will need to be turned under and fastened with appliqué stitches.
4 Pick up all the pieces again and fasten back the raw edges which do need to be turned under using one of these methods:
● Stay stitch along them keeping slightly inside fold line. Clip close to the stitching curves.
● Place the template on the wrong side of the corresponding cut-fabric piece. Press the raw edges back over the template, carefully folding back along the marked fold line. Clip the curves.
● Fold raw edges back by hand and tack. Clip any curves before tacking to ease the fold around curved lines.
5 Pin or tack the shirt piece to the background material.
6 Now stitch it to the background material using small hemming or blind hemming stitches. You could also use a running stitch, which will look like a row of quilting.
7 Appliqué the overalls on top of the shirt, leaving the bottoms of the trouser legs free. Push the raw edges of the tops of the shoes under the trouser legs, and fold the edges of the trouser bottoms under making sure that they still cover raw edges of the shoe tops. Secure the folded edge with blind hemming stitches or one of the other stitches mentioned above.
8 Secure the folded edges of the shoes.
9 Stitch on the hat so that it covers the raw edges on top of the overalls' shoulder straps.
10 Add details with embroidery if desired.

Machine appliqué

1 Cut the appliqué exactly on the pencil line marked by tracing round the template. The raw edges will not be folded under, but will be covered by machine satin stitches.
2 Tack your appliqué onto your background fabric by hand or machine.
3 Use machine satin stitch to cover the raw edges and hold the appliqué in place.

A useful sewing aid when doing appliqué work is Bondaweb. This is a paper-backed adhesive which holds fast when ironed on to material. It can be used to hold the appliqué in place while you stitch round it and also prevents fraying

When sewing appliqués onto lightweight fabrics, place a piece of tissue paper under the appliqué and background material. Sew right through it when you appliqué and tear off from the back when sewing is completed

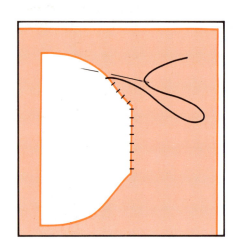

Broderie perse

Another type of appliqué involves cutting out printed motifs such as flowers, fruit and birds from fabric and appliquéing these onto a background fabric. This method of appliqué (also known as broderie perse) was especially popular during the 18th century when printed fabrics were scarce, since, by this method, small amounts of printed fabric could be used to decorate a large quilt.

If you'd like to try appliquéing motifs from printed fabric, make sure you leave a margin of $\frac{1}{4}$ to $\frac{1}{2}$ inch beyond the edge of the motif when you cut out the design. This margin will be folded under to hide the raw edges.

Reverse appliqué

As the name suggests, reverse appliqué is just the opposite of appliqué. As we've just seen, appliqué involves stitching small pieces of fabric onto a larger background fabric. In reverse appliqué, rather than adding pieces on top of one another, layers of fabric are cut away, revealing the material below.

Reverse appliqué is a technique practised with great skill by the Kuna Indian women of the San Blas Islands, off the coast of Panama. During the 19th century, traders brought the Indians fabric and sewing supplies and the Indians translated their colourful body paintings into reverse appliqué designs, called molas, which they then used to decorate clothing. A typical mola is made with two to four layers of fabric, placed on top of one another. Often the bottom layer is pieced from several different-coloured fabrics, giving the effect of an even greater number of layers being used. For the same reason, appliqués are often added to the top layer of the mola. Embroidery stitches are used to add details.

Reverse appliqué is an interesting and challenging technique that is not often seen today. Terrie Mangat, a quilt designer from Cincinnati, explains why she began using the technique:

I think the first time I used reverse appliqué was when I wanted to put some images on a quilt. I started to appliqué some little cows in a field in a picture of a farm. All the cows were getting stretched out of shape and I thought there must be a better way to do it. I think I must have seen some molas from South America, and I decided that that technique would probably work better in getting finer detail. I tried it and found it did work better for me.

Terrie often uses old X-ray film instead of cardboard for her templates, as it never loses its edge however many times you trace round it. This would be difficult for most people to obtain, but you could try using stiff graphic art film (available from large art shops) instead. Terrie continues:

Clipping at the curves is the most important part in the technique that I use, because if you don't clip at the right spot, it's not going to bend the way you want it to. You'll have a straight line instead of a curve if you don't clip. I clip right out to the line. You have to have scissors that clip sharp all the way out to the point. If you use scissors that aren't very sharp at the point, you may as well forget about doing it, because you won't be able to get the detail. I don't need to stitch under all of the raw edges. I stitch only under the edges that will show. Then I turn all of those raw edges on top underneath. First I pin them in place. . . Then I use my needle as a tool to help turn under the edges to get the curves. I turn it right on the little line so that you can't see the line anymore, or just barely. The bend of the fabric is right on the line. I turn it under with my needle and then I just take tiny stitches right at the edge. I come up right through the end of the fold and then I go back down right next to it. My sister does a little running stitch right underneath the turned-under fabric. That probably is the traditional way to do it, but my way works better for me.

For more information on molas, see: 'A Trip to the San Blas Islands' by Donna Renshaw, *Quilter's Newsletter Magazine*, April 1977, pp8–9 (Also see Bibliography)

See Terrie Mangat in 'The Meeting Place' *Quilter's Newsletter Magazine*, February 1981, p26 (Also see p2)

Quilts in the TV series

CHAROLAIS CALVES©
Calf silhouettes done in vibrant combinations of colour and pattern.

GIRAFFES©
The design was inspired by a piece of African material which Terrie set into the middle section of the quilt. She used reverse appliqué to copy the giraffe shape from the printed fabric.

Illustrated in: *Quilter's Newsletter Magazine*, February 1981, p26

DEAR HARTS AND OLD CHINTZ©
This quilt uses a variety of materials such as glazed cotton and gold lamé that catch and reflect the light. Twenty-five hearts were cut out of the top layer of red chintz and reverse appliquéd to a bottom layer pieced of blue cotton, flowered chintz and gold lamé. Deer silhouettes were appliquéd to the hearts at the centre and outside edges.

Illustrated in: *Quilter's Newsletter Magazine*, September 1980, p9

SCHOOL DAYS©
This quilt combines the techniques of piecing, appliqué and reverse appliqué. Terrie used almost entirely patterned fabric throughout this quilt, carefully combining prints of different size and scale. The running figures of children were, like the deer seen in the previous quilt, inspired by a street sign—this one for a school crossing.

Illustrated in: *Quilter's Newsletter Magazine*, February 1981, p26

DEER SPIRITS©	Terrie Mangat
	3 Madison Lane
	Cincinnati
	OH 45208, USA

Here the whole quilt is treated as a picture to create a surrealistic scene of hunters, deer and restless deer spirits.

Contemporary appliqué quilts shown:

IVY-COVERED WALL©	Michael James

Illustrated in: *The Second Quiltmaker's Handbook*, Michael James

See: *Fiberarts* magazine, 'Jo Diggs' September/October 1976, pp24–29

QUILTED JACKET©	Jo Diggs
QUILTED DRESS PANEL©	Box 4240
AUTUMN SCENE©	Winslow
ROCK WALL LANDSCAPE©	ME 04902, USA
MILL TOWN©	

Illustrated in: *Quilter's Newsletter Magazine*, October 1980, p37

MALLARDS II©	Nell Cogswell
MALLARDS©	Box 99
CAPE PORPOISE QUILT©	Carlisle
	MA 01741, USA

THE QUILTMAKERS©	Carolyn Muller
	380 Oliver Road
	Cincinnati
	OH 45215, USA

Bibliography

Auld, Rhoda L. *Molas*
Van Nostrand Reinhold Co, New York and Wokingham, 1977

Laury, Jean Ray. *Quilts and Coverlets: A Contemporary Approach*
Van Nostrand Reinhold Co, New York and Wokingham, 1971

Machine and hand appliqué

Parker, Ann and Neal, Avon. *Molas, Folk Art of the Kuna Indians*
Crown Publishers, Inc, New York, 1977

Patera, Charlotte. *The Mola Pattern Book*
Patera Pattern Press, Box 886, Novato, CA 94947, USA (by post)

Reverse appliqué

Puls, Herta. *The Art of Cutwork and Applique, Historic, Modern and Kuna Indian*
Charles T Branford Co, New York, 1978

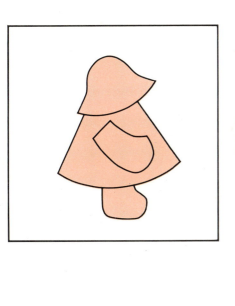

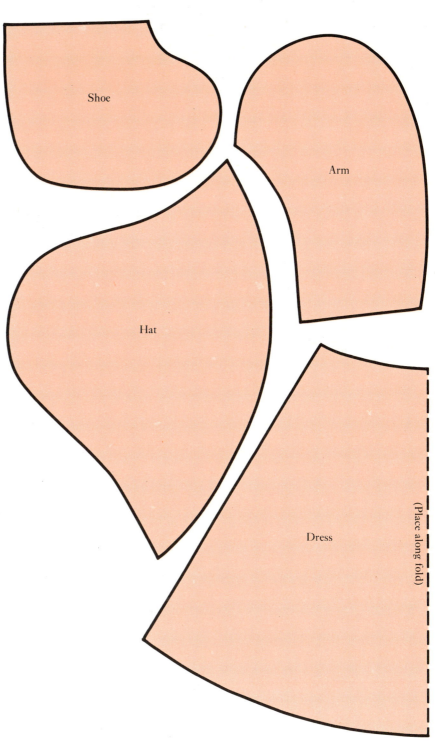

Shoe

Arm

Hat

Dress

(Place along fold)

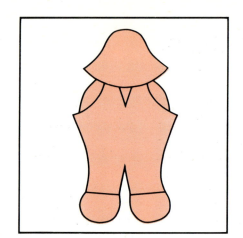

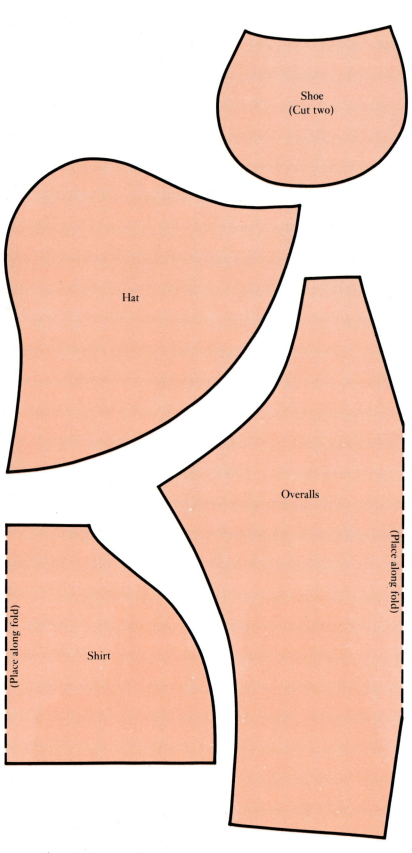

Shoe
(Cut two)

Hat

Overalls

(Place along fold)

Shirt

(Place along fold)

GROUP-MADE QUILTS

For a good discussion of album quilts, see: *Quilts in America* by the Orlofskys, pp233–39

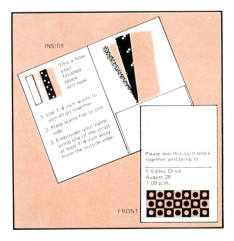

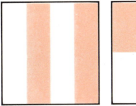

Rail fence   4-patch

Split block

The Hudson River Quilt has been featured in many books and magazines. One is *America's Quilts and Coverlets* by Safford and Bishop, p219

Another interesting idea to come from across the Atlantic is that of group-made quilts. In the late 1840s and 1850s in the USA, album quilts became extremely popular, especially in Delaware and Maryland. For these quilts, a block would be made by each member of a group and the blocks then sewn together and quilted by the whole group at a social gathering. The quilt was often made as a gift to be presented to someone to remind them of the group concerned. These old album quilts are extremely elaborate; it's as if each block-maker was trying to outdo the others in design and craftsmanship.

If you like the idea of organising a similar project, you can, of course, use very simple designs for your group to make up. Here are some ideas for making a group quilt:

1   Invite your group to bring along a pre-determined number of squares of material already cut to the correct size. Stipulate a material that is easy to sew, such as a polyester/cotton mixture. When you are all together, decide on the arrangement of squares and hand-sew the blocks together. Either quilt the top at the same gathering or do it yourself afterwards.

2   Try making a contemporary autograph quilt. Send squares of fabric to your guests. Ask them to embroider their blocks with their names (or a message) and return them to you. Set the blocks together, tack the top to your wadding and backing and put it into a quilting frame. Ask the guests to come round on a certain date to quilt it.

3   Send out pre-cut fabric pieces with your invitations, along with easy-to-follow directions for making up the pieced block. Ask your guests to return the finished blocks in advance so that you can make up the quilt top and get it ready for quilting. Some easy block designs to try are 'rail fence', '4-patch' and 'split block' (illustrated left).

Making a group-made appliqué quilt like the old album quilts requires a lot more planning and technical skill than the ideas suggested here. But the resulting quilts are a great deal more personal since each block can be used to illustrate people, places or events meaningful to the group or the recipient.

In 1976, in America, there was a big upsurge in the production of such group-made quilts to commemorate the Bicentennial Celebration. Thousands of groups made quilts in honour of their own city or region and many of them are extremely beautiful.

Part of the reason for the rebirth of interest in quilt-making at this time was the fame of one special quilt that captured the imagination of many people. That quilt was the 'Hudson River Quilt'.

Hudson River Quilt

The Hudson River Quilt was the idea of Irene Preston Miller of Croton-On-Hudson, New York. In 1969 she combined her interest in needlework and local conservation with the idea of making a quilt to raise funds to aid in cleaning up the Hudson River. Twenty-nine women joined her in the project. Each woman designed and appliquéd a block based upon the theme of the Hudson River. The women worked independently, without seeing one another's blocks until they were sewn together to make the quilt top.

The finished blocks were joined together, laid on wadding and backing and quilted. Most of the block-makers were new to quilting and produced quilting stitches that, as Irene Preston Miller says, look fine from the front, but could stand improvement on the back. After it was completed, the Hudson River Quilt was seen throughout the country in exhibitions, book illustrations and postcards. It was the first of the thousands of pictorial group-made quilts sewn during the 1970s to commemorate the Bicentennial, and was often used as a model.

Hudson River Quilt

Oberlin Quilt

There's a direct link between the Hudson River Quilt and another famous contemporary US quilt, the Oberlin Quilt. When quilt-maker Ricky Clark of Oberlin received a postcard showing the Hudson River Quilt she decided to organise her own quilt-making group. This resulted in the Oberlin Quilt, completed in 1974. It now hangs in the Oberlin College library. Ricky Clark describes how the quilt came into being:

How did the group get together to make a quilt?
Three of us just randomly asked people we thought might be interested. Another community might do it through a church group or any established organisation. Few of our group were quilters. Most of them had made their own clothes, but that was all the sewing experience they had. We trained ourselves and each other. I ran a series of appliqué workshops for people who hadn't had that experience. Another member of our group who had done quilting ran quilting workshops.

How did the workshops operate?
We brought materials for them to cut. In the appliqué workshop, I had people cut different shapes because appliquéing along the grain of the fabric is different from appliquéing elaborate curves. I tried to cover all the technical problems that might arise when doing appliqué.

How did you decide on the colours and designs for the quilt?
We knew that we'd have to hold the quilt together visually because there were so many different scenes. Most people seemed to have sky or grass in their block. So we bought two shades of green and two of blue and asked people who needed blue and green if they would use the fabrics we bought. When all the squares were completed, we laid them out on tablecloths and sheets in different colours so that we could choose a background colour which would be the lattice strip framework for the squares.

Did everyone design their own blocks?
Yes, and I feel strongly about that. I know a lot of groups have an artist design blocks and the women just do the technical work. We found it was much more personal, much more fun, for each woman to design her own block. And we discovered that we could, in fact, do our own designing.

What kind of problems might arise in working with a group?
The more problems you can anticipate the better it is. One problem is quality control. What are you going to do if one woman comes in with a block that she thinks is absolutely lovely and really isn't up to the quilt? You're going to have to cope with this, and if you can anticipate it, you'll avoid a lot of pain. Also, in case someone did not get her block made or dropped out of the group, I made an extra square to go into the quilt. As it was, it didn't need to be used, so I took it home, framed it, and I have it on the wall of my studio. Also, sometimes someone gets into trouble on a particular square. We were able to involve the whole group in solving this. One girl, for instance, who had a difficult object to depict, discovered that trying to make a two-dimensional surface look three dimensional is a challenge . . . She was not satisfied with her block and brought it in. A lot of constructive helpful suggestions came out of that. She redid the square in a way that was much more satisfactory to her.

Working with a group must have been an interesting project in itself.
It certainly was. I made a lot of new friends. We had a wonderful time together and we got involved in each other's project. For instance, one woman represented a night that occurs every year in Oberlin when the public square is hung with Japanese lanterns. She wanted psychedelic fabrics. So everyone in the group was on the lookout for psychedelic fabrics for this one person, even though we were all working on other problems.

Beloit College Quilt

Beloit Quilt

The Oberlin Quilt, in turn, has inspired many other groups to make quilts commemorating regions or institutions. When Marrlyn Garret of Beloit, Wisconsin, saw a postcard of the Oberlin Quilt in 1975 she interested members of the Beloit College Women's Club in making a quilt based on the theme of Beloit College. The quilt was completed in the spring of 1978 and now hangs in the college library. When Marrlyn decided to organise a quilt-making group, she had specific ideas about how she wanted the finished quilt to look. She decided that she wanted muted reds, greens, blues and yellows rather than stronger primary colours. She began assembling her fabric by choosing the greens, which she thought would be the hardest shades to blend successfully. She also decided to use an off-white rather than a true white, which she felt would stand out too starkly from the rest of the materials.

All the fabric was purchased before the quilt was started, and as each person selected fabrics for her block, a record was kept of the colours and prints used. In this way, Marrlyn hoped to be able to check to see that the colours were being evenly distributed throughout the quilt top. It was also suggested to the block-makers that each block be designed to resemble a scene, looking as though the picture continued off on both sides of the block.

When all the blocks had been appliquéd, they were ready to be quilted. Instead of being joined to make one large quilt top before quilting, each block was quilted separately, and then joined with lattice strips. Rather than the usual method of stitching lines $\frac{1}{8}$ inch away from the appliqué, the blocks were quilted right along the appliqué edge so they fell into the area where the appliqué was folded under, a method that is sometimes referred to as quilting 'in the ditch'. In this way, the quilting was not seen as lines of stitches but still made the appliquéd area puff out.

Maumee Quilt

The Beloit College Quilt centred around the theme of the college. Other group quilts are based on some particular aspect of the institution or city for which they're made. The Maumee Quilt, made to honour the city of Maumee, Ohio, depicts historic homes in the city. Forty-two women, led by Fran Ochenas and Judi Warren, worked on the quilt from February 1975 to May 1976. Some of the women made blocks showing their own homes while the remainder selected historic houses that they admired from the area.

The Maumee Quilt was dedicated to earlier quilt-makers and to recording, in appliqué, the appearance of homes that had, in most cases, stood for more than 100 years and which might not exist for 100 more. To document the quilt, a detailed brochure was printed showing a photograph of the quilt, giving a brief history of each house depicted and information about the quilt-makers.

Cincinnati Quilt

As interest in quilting grew during the 1970s, more and more people enrolled in quilting classes offered by quilting shops, museums and adult education departments. As part of these classes, students often worked on individual blocks which were combined with others to make one large quilt. One such quilt now hangs in the Cincinnati Art Museum.

The Cincinnati Quilt was the idea of Betty Alfers, an adult education quilting teacher who began the project with 24 students in the autumn of 1973. The quilt was completed in March 1974 and was presented to the City of Cincinnati at a city council meeting. The quilt is composed of 28 appliquéd blocks depicting a wide variety of symbols and landmarks for which the city is known.

The Louisville Quilts

Even after the Bicentennial was over, groups continued to be interested in making commemorative quilts in America.

In 1979, Roberta Williams, Director of the Louisville Art Gallery, came up with the idea of several quilting workshops and lectures to interest people in making quilts in honour of the combined Louisville/Jefferson County Bicentennial. The interest in the project was amazing. By the autumn of the following year, more than 1000 people from the ages of 4 to 80 had worked on one of the 49 quilts that were made. The quilts were all put on display in an exhibition entitled 'Louisville Quilts', but have now gone their separate ways to hang in schools and homes, or be tucked away. But plans have been made for them to be brought out in another 100 years when they again will hang together in an exhibition, possibly along with new quilts from the 21st century.

Quilts in the TV series

1976 MEDLEY–BICENTENNIAL FRIENDSHIP QUILT	Sophie Crittenden 84 Wildwood Drive Mansfield OH 44907, USA
BOWLING GREEN BICENTENNIAL QUILT	

Bibliography

Holland, Nina. *Pictorial Quilting*
A S Barnes and Co, Inc, San Diego, 1978; Thomas Yoseloff Ltd, London, 1978 (now out of print but may be available through your library)

Safford, C L and Bishop, R C. *America's Quilts and Coverlets*
E P Dutton, New York, 1972

See: 'Louisville Quilts' by Katy Christopherson, *Quilt* magazine, Summer 1981, pp8–9

Postcards and notecards of *Landmarks, Churches* and *Balloons* quilts can be ordered from: Main Library, 301 York St, Louisville, KY 40203, USA

Quilt blocks were exchanged by post for this friendship quilt

A large number of group-made appliqué quilts are discussed and illustrated in this book

Balloon Race Quilt

Churches of Louisville

9

PICTURE QUILTS–ED LARSON

George Washington Quilt—Larson

See also: 'Creating Fabric Pictures' Edward Larson, *Quilter's Newsletter Magazine*, March 1979, p8

Some designers use their quilt top to tell a story or to illustrate a single scene by using appliqué. One such designer is Edward Larson from Illinois, USA. Ed first became interested in quilts as a contemporary folk artist (he is also a wood-carver), and he had a one-man show of his work in New York in 1980. His designs have a whimsical quality and are often humorous, such as his 'Fight of the Century' quilt, which shows the artist knocking out Mohammed Ali!

Ed gives workshops in America on how to make a picture quilt. Here are some of his suggestions:

1   Decide on the basic idea or story that you'd like to show. A quilt can tell a family story or just be a depiction of people and places that mean something to you.

2   Accumulate photographs, magazine pictures, or the actual objects that you'd like to represent on your quilt.

3   Work out your design on an 8×10 inch sheet of paper. First, find a place for the largest image. (You don't need to fill in the whole quilt with images—perhaps you'd prefer to concentrate on the centre and surround the centre with borders.)

4   Draw the images very simply using large basic shapes—circles for heads, rectangles for necks, arms and legs, for example. Details can be added later with embroidery.

5   Don't worry about putting all the images of people, houses, animals, etc. together in one scene with a horizon and showing perspective. Take a tip from crazy quilts (see p49) and try placing each image on its own crazy-quilt-like patch. Then just fit the patches together. Part of the beauty of the picture can be the randomness of the background design.

6   When the main area of the quilt has been sketched, develop border designs to frame the picture. One idea is to use traditional blocks in the corners and simple strips along the edges of the quilt.

7   Once your drawing has been completed, make some photocopies of it and try out colours in a variety of ways.

8   Enlarge your 8×10 paper sketch onto a big sheet of wrapping paper (or tape several pieces of paper together) to the size you want your finished quilt to be. To enlarge the drawing:
●   Either draw a grid of $\frac{1}{2}$ inch squares across your 8×10 paper sketch, and draw a grid of 6-inch squares onto your large sheet of paper. Transfer the pattern from your small sketch by drawing each line from the small squares onto the corresponding squares on the large sheet.
●   Or photograph your drawing with slide film. Project your slide onto the large sheet of paper and then draw on top of the projected lines.

9   Now use the *large paper drawing* (never cut up your original drawing) as a pattern by:
●   Either cutting up the paper and using the individual sections as pattern pieces. Pin each paper pattern piece to the material and cut the fabric $\frac{1}{4}$ inch away from the pattern edge. (This will allow you $\frac{1}{4}$ inch to fold under when appliquéing.)
●   Or laying tracing paper over the large pattern and making a copy which can then be cut up into pieces.

10   Appliqué and piece the fabric together to make the quilt top.

Be sure to place your name and the date the quilt was made somewhere on the quilt. You could put it on the quilt back or work it into the design of the quilt top. You may also want to add other information such as where the quilt was made, or, if you're telling a story in the quilt, you can identify what is going on and who is being depicted. This makes the quilt more meaningful to others.

Seven Suitors Quilt—Larson

Quilts in the TV series

Illustrated in: 'Pictorial Quilts: A New Trend?' *Quilter's Newsletter Magazine*, December 1976, p16

CAT QUILT	Ed Larson
EMANCIPATION QUILT	208 E Broadway
	Libertyville
	IL 60048, USA

Ed Larson is represented by:	Monique Knowlton Gallery
	New York, USA

Energy Quilt—Larson

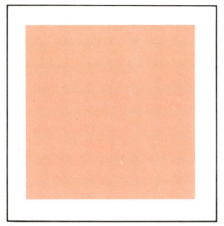

Square

Diamond

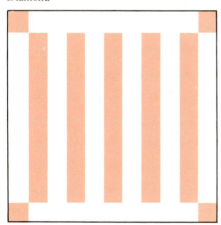

Bars

Sunshine and Shadow

Another type of quilt design which originated in America and in which interest has revived recently is that developed by the Amish religious sect. They used simple pieced designs and strong colour contrast to great effect.

The Amish have an interesting history. In 1693 the Swiss Bishop Jacob Amman broke with the Mennonite movement, which wanted to follow a slightly less strict form of 'shunning' or total avoidance of a person who broke any of the Church's rules. Amman wanted to adhere to the old rigorous practices of the Church. His followers became known as the Amish, after his name. The earliest Amish settlers came to America around 1727 and settled on the fertile farmland of Pennysylvania. As the number of Amish grew, groups split and in the early 19th century, many moved farther west to Ohio and Indiana.

The most traditional Amish avoid any dependence on the outside world. They have rejected such modern products of progress as cars, telephones, electricity and modern clothes. Amish quilts are plain and utilitarian, pieced out of large straight-edged units rather than the smaller and often curved pieces which make up traditional non-Amish quilts (and which would have been considered frivolous by the Amish). Patterned material was rejected because it was too worldly, and white was avoided as it was a colour reserved for funerals.

The quilts considered typically Amish in design are those that were made in Pennsylvania.

Pennsylvania Amish quilts

Some of the general characteristics of Pennsylvania Amish quilts are that they are:

- Square in shape.
- Designed from the centre out towards the edges.
- Surrounded by wide borders edged with narrow binding.
- Composed of one overall design rather than blocks.
- Quilted in elaborate patterns.

There are four basic Pennsylvania Amish quilt designs:

Square
a simple one-colour square of material which is an example of a one-piece quilt. Borders could be added to this square, with or without corner blocks.

Diamond
the diamond design typically has many borders surrounding the central panel, and colours often repeat in different areas of the quilt.

Bars
a strip quilt surrounded by borders.

Sunshine and Shadow
small squares arranged to form diamonds of colour that radiate out from the quilt's centre.

Designing Sunshine and Shadow

1 On graph paper draw a square that represents the finished size of your project. Make sure that you work with an *uneven* number of graph squares. (For example, you could let one square on graph paper stand for 1 inch on a cushion cover and draw a unit 13 squares across and 13 squares down. If you're designing a quilt, let the graph paper squares stand for 3 or 4 inches in your finished quilt.)
2 Find the graph paper square at the centre and colour it in.
3 With another colour, shade in the squares directly above, below and to the sides of the centre square.

4 Continue forming rings of colour as shown in the illustration.
5 Use this graph paper design to tell you how many squares of each colour you need to cut, and in which order they should be sewn.

Sewing Sunshine and Shadow

1 Make a square template to whatever size your small graph paper squares represent with an added $\frac{1}{4}$ inch on all sides for seam allowance. For a cushion, you might make a template $1\frac{1}{2}$ inches square; for a quilt, perhaps $3\frac{1}{2}$ inches square.
2 Following the graph paper design, mark and cut out the required fabric squares.
3 Sew up the squares in rows, beginning at the top left of your design, and sewing in the colour order indicated on your graph paper design. Pin a sequence number onto each row as it is completed to avoid confusion when you come to sew up the rows.
4 Press all the rows, ironing the seams flat.
5 Sew the rows together in number order, carefully pinning through each matched pair of seams so that they will line up.
6 Press the finished top; add borders if desired and quilt. (Quilting is traditionally done around each square or diagonally across it.)

Quilt exhibition

'Amish Quilts' Miami University Art Museum (June 28–August 24, 1980). For more information on the exhibition, contact: Bill Osmun, Comprehensive Exhibition Services, 453 Sycamore Rd, Santa Monica, CA 90402, USA

American quilt collectors such as Gail van der Hoof and Jonathon Holstein have helped increase awareness of Amish quilts by organising exhibitions of them both in the USA and in Europe. The quilts in their collection are mainly from Pennsylvania and were made by the Old Order Amish. Edna Carter Southard from the Miami University Museum in Ohio was one of the people involved in the exhibition of Amish quilts mounted there in 1980 and is very familiar with the history of this sect:

What aspects of Amish culture are reflected in their quilts?
The Amish believe that their clothing is an outward manifestation of their beliefs, so they wear dark sombre clothing and avoid patterned material and the use of appliqué (so that one doesn't waste any material). There is also a love of geometry which comes through. That is typical of their lives, too . . . There are only a few basic patterns that the Amish use, and the Diamond pattern is one of the most frequent ones that appear. There are just a few colours that are used . . . and the pattern is very simple and very geometric. But the stitchery itself is quite elaborate and beautiful. It's done with a template, of course. Some of the women became so skilled that they could do it freehand.

Were there some quilting patterns that a family would adopt as their own?
Yes, there were. In fact, there would be variations done by a mother for her three daughters. There's a case that is recorded where the pattern was exactly the same but a little section of a different colour would be put in. Nearly all of the quilts use a dark thread. And they don't vary the thread, despite the fact that the colour of material varies. Sunshine and Shadow is another basic Amish pattern and was used in one of the latest of the quilts in the exhibition dating from about 1935.

Is that the same pattern that non-Amish people would do in calicos and call Around the World?
Yes, it is. Many people are reminded of Op Art when they look at Sunshine and Shadow quilts. One of my favourite Amish quilts has a saw-tooth diamond design, which uses just two colours, blue and red. The quilter just used naturally dyed wool, in contrast to some who used synthetic dyes as well as synthetic material. It's beautifully done and balanced and designed. The sense of geometry, the sense of design, is a way in which the Amish women beautified their homes. And I think that this quilt is particularly expressive of that.

Midwestern Amish quilts

Darwin Bearley, Quilts & Country, 98 Beck Ave, Akron, Ohio 44302, USA

The Amish quilts of Pennsylvania are more conservative than those made in the Midwest of the USA. Darwin Bearley, a quilt dealer from Akron, Ohio, is a specialist in Ohio Amish quilts.

What is the difference between Pennsylvania and Ohio Amish quilts?
I think the first thing you notice is the shape of the overall quilt. Most Pennsylvania Amish quilts are square. In Ohio, most quilts, with few exceptions, are more rectangular. The other main difference, again with exceptions, is that the Pennsylvania quilts have minimal patterns. The pieces tend to be quite large and the pattern very simple, as in the typical Lancaster county Amish quilts of Pennsylvania.

In Ohio we tend to find that the Amish used more traditional quilt patterns—everything from a commonly known Double Wedding Ring to the Log Cabin pattern to just about everything that was ever invented as a quilt pattern, plus some unusual pieces. The other thing that's probably different is that technically, because of the size of the pattern in the open field, Lancaster quilts tend to be quilted more fancily. Ohio quilts use more outline quilting around the individual pieces in the quilt. They're not quite as delicate as the Pennsylvania quilts.

Another minor difference one notices is the border widths. Lancaster quilts tend to be very wide with wide inner borders. Ohio quilts have a narrower border with a narrower inner border. And the binding itself is different. The Ohio pieces tend to have a thinner, maybe a quarter inch, or three-eighths inch wide binding. The Lancaster Amish quilts tend to have maybe an inch, or inch-and-a-half binding.

Pennsylvania Amish quilts are rarely done in blocks. Ohio Amish quilts use more of a traditional type of pattern. You'll find all types of colours in Ohio. But during periods of quilt-making in Ohio, you notice things such as in the pre-1900 quilts, you'll find a lot of brown used, more earthy colours, especially in the background. From 1900 to 1925, roughly, they tend to use a lot of black in the background colours. And from then to the present time, they tend to get into more pastel colours. A quilt, referred to among the Amish as a Railroad Crossing pattern, uses both black and pastels. It is unique to the Ohio Amish. I have never seen the pattern used in any non-Amish quilt or any Amish quilt outside of Ohio.

Has the popularity of Amish quilts affected the way they're being made?
I think it's kind of a sad note that the current quilts being produced, unless they are specifically ordered, tend not to have any Amish characteristics at all. They use printed fabric. They use some double knit, some horribly woven fabric, usually from fabric mills that they get scraps from. They use whatever they can find. Amish quilts, as most people think of them, are not being made any more. There are weak examples. The craftsmanship is not there. The whole idea of what their grandparents were into has been lost. . . I think it's an economic thing. Years ago, nobody was really interested in these dark black and brown quilts. So to make money, they started making quilts that the non-Amish would buy. These were quilts with printed fabrics and lighter colours and more 'cute' things, as opposed to strong, graphic, more contemporary things. And I think that's probably the main reason the quilt has changed among the Amish.

Quilted Weaving—Spaeth

Spectrum III—Randles

Quilts in the TV series

AMISH TOUCAN c	Marjorie Claybrook
AMISH BARS c	Sue Hoyt 380 E Northwood Columbus OH 43201, USA
AMISH-STYLE QUILTED JACKET c	Judy Mathieson 5802 Jumilla Avenue Woodland Hills CA 91367, USA
HANDY ANDY ADAPTATION QUILTED WEAVING c UNTITLED c	Peggy Spaeth 1672 Eddington Cleveland Heights OH 44118, USA
SPECTRUM III c	Virginia Randles 6 Strouds Run Athens OH 45701, USA

Bibliography

Bishop, Robert. *New Discoveries in American Quilts*
E P Dutton, New York, 1975

Haders, Phyllis. *Sunshine and Shadow: The Amish and Their Quilts*
Universe Books, New York, 1976

Holstein, Jonathon. *The Pieced Quilt: An American Design Tradition*
New York Graphic Society Ltd, 34 Beacon St, Boston, MA 02154, 1973

CRAZY QUILTS

The crazy quilt is one of the best known types of quilts and since crazy quilt design depends so much on the artistic ability of the maker, some of the best, and some of the worst-designed quilts are crazy quilts. Crazy quilts differ from traditional cotton quilts both in their design and use:

Pieced cotton quilt	*Crazy quilt*
Use	
Bed-cover;	Sofa, bed or table covering;
● Washable, durable and made for warmth	● Not washable, fragile and made for show
● Three layers, quilted	● Two layers, no wadding, tied
Design	
● Regular, predictable; each block has same design	● Irregular, unpredictable; each block is different
● Straight lines predominate	● Curved or jagged lines predominate
● Stitches holding blocks together are functional, unnoticeable	● Stitches holding quilt together are functional but also very noticeable and decorative

At the end of the 19th century both these types of quilts were being made, but the really popular quilt of the period was the crazy quilt.

The origin of crazy quilt design is still uncertain. Some believe that the crazy quilt style of joining irregular pieces of fabric was the earliest way of making quilts. Others think that it originated when irregular patches were used to cover worn spots on old quilts. As more and more patches were added, the worn quilt gradually began to look like a crazy quilt. There are no crazy quilts (as we know them) from the 18th century in existence, however, so the theories of early crazy quilts remain unproven.

Whatever its origins, the crazy quilt reflected the popular taste of the late 19th century in Britain and America which favoured an eclectic mixture of styles, patterns, textures and colours in all aspects of the decorative arts. Furniture was made of dark wood, which was then heavily carved. Table-tops were covered with lace cloths and objects of all kinds. Walls were hung with richly patterned and flocked wallpaper and paintings in intricately carved frames. Rugs in a wide variety of designs covered the floor. This profusion of pattern and texture may seem overdone to our eyes more used to the spare, clean lines of modern design, but these rich Victorian furnishings represented to their owners the security and prosperity reached after years of struggle.

At the height of its popularity, crazy quilting was used to cover cushions, benches and all kinds of decorative objects.

How to make a crazy quilt block

Take advantage of the interesting shapes of left-over scraps of material for crazy quilt blocks

There are several ways of making a crazy quilt block. Here are two. Both begin with a piece of fabric the size of the finished square. This is called a foundation block and can be made from any medium-weight fabric, such as a soft cotton.

Hand method
1 Make sure that the material you are going to use has been pressed since it is hard to press a finished block.
2 Either start from the middle of the block, or from one corner.
3 Lay pieces of fabric (any kind—wool, velvet, cotton, silk, etc.) onto

A crazy quilt can also be made on one large foundation piece backing the whole quilt

a foundation backing, overlapping their edges by at least $\frac{1}{2}$ inch.

The best way to learn new embroidery stitches for use on a crazy quilt is by practising, using a book to help you. Try: *Crazy Quilt Stitches*, Dorothy Bond

For more details on this machine-sewn crazy quilt technique, see: *The Contemporary Crazy Quilt Project Book*, Dixie Haywood

This method produces a block with primarily straight lines. You can add curving lines by appliquéing patches with curved edges

Patterns for embroidery were sold for many of the most popular motifs

Painting on velvet was a popular pastime, and many crazy quilts contain painted patches

4   When all the foundation backing is covered and you have found an arrangement that you like, pin the pieces down.
5   Beginning at one corner, pin the raw edges under. Let overlapping patches cover the raw edges beneath.
6   Use embroidery stitches to hold the raw edges under and fasten the patches to the foundation backing.

Machine method
This is a quick way of sewing crazy quilt blocks. For a quilted look, place a square of wadding on top of the foundation block and sew through both layers.
1   As in the hand-sewn example, make sure your fabric has been pressed.
2   Begin by sewing the first patch in the centre of the block. Use a straight machine stitch and sew $\frac{1}{8}$ inch from the raw edge of the patch, directly through the wadding and/or foundation block.
3   Add the next patch by placing it on top of the first patch, right sides of the material together, and lining up the raw edges as you would if sewing a seam. Sew $\frac{1}{8}$ to $\frac{1}{4}$ inch away from the raw edges. Fold the patch over so the right side is face upwards.
4   Add the rest of the patches in turn—each patch will cover the raw edges of the preceding one. If any raw edges are left showing in places, turn them under and sew by hand.
5   If any bare sections of the foundation backing are left showing, cover them by appliquéing small patches over the area.
6   Finish with hand or machine embroidery.

Use for clothing

Since crazy quilt blocks grow to fit the shape of the original foundation backing, they can be made in any size or shape and are, therefore, ideal for use in clothing. Just begin with a foundation shape the size of the pattern piece and bear in mind washing or dry-cleaning requirements when selecting fabrics.

Crazy quilt motifs

Making crazy quilt squares edged with embroidery is just the first step in making a crazy quilt. The quilt-maker looks upon her crazy quilt top as a painter would look at a blank canvas—it is a surface waiting to be decorated. In Victorian times, the more decoration that could be applied to the surface, the more successful the crazy quilt was considered to be.

The motifs that women embroidered on these quilt tops reflected the things that were important in their lives as well as the fashionable trends of the day. One of these trends was an interest in anything oriental. This interest grew as a result of the opening of trade with Japan in the mid-19th century and also displays of Japanese art. Suddenly the use of fans in quilt designs became popular. This interest in oriental designs was also responsible for the frequent use of the butterfly as a decorative motif. At the same time as the American artist James McNeil Whistler was using the butterfly as a symbol for his signature on prints, late 19th century American quilt-makers were decorating their quilts with embroidered and appliquéd butterfly designs.

On the whole, the vogue for Japanese design encouraged the use of curving, sinuous lines and off-centre, irregular compositions in all the arts of the period. Crazy quilts also reflect the popularity of the illustrator Kate Greenaway in the 1880s. Greenaway's drawings showed children playing happily in rustic settings, dressed in fashions from a century earlier. It is common to find scenes adapted from Kate Greenaway drawings, embroidered onto quilts, and her style of dressing girls in long, high-waisted dresses with caps or sun-bonnets is a primary source of the 'Sunbonnet Sue' patterns that are still popular today in a variation called 'Holly Hobbie'.

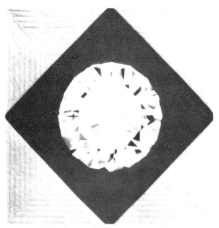
Diamond — Cogswell

Two-tiered Town — Cohen

Flowers have always been important sources of quilt design, and they were especially popular during this period. Certain flowers were given symbolic meanings that conveyed a message. The lily stood for purity, forget-me-nots for remembrance and the rose for love. Crazy quilts often served as a kind of fabric scrapbook of remembrances, preserving such things as pressed fabric flowers from an old dress or hat, or commemorative ribbons from an event. Names and autographs of friends or celebrities show up frequently as do popular sayings or scenes from books.

Common to all crazy quilts is the use of materials which had good light-reflecting qualities. In the Victorian parlour, the heavy curtains were generally kept closed to keep sunlight from fading the furnishings, so the beads and golden thread used on silks and satins caught and reflected interior light in the dim room.

Tacking quilt top to backing

After the crazy quilt top had been pieced together and embroidered, the back, showing knots and stitches, was covered by a lining. The method used to attach this backing material to the crazy quilt top is basically the same as tieing (see p9), but the tie shows on the back of the quilt rather than the front.

Caroline Shine, who is responsible for the Cincinnati Art Museum's collection of costumes and textiles, gives these tips on the care and storage of crazy quilts:

How are the quilts in the museum's collection stored?
We keep them folded in drawers. Ideally, you should have one quilt to the drawer, but few people have that kind of space. You want as few folds as possible. If you have to fold a quilt, it's a good idea to put in a little padding where it's folded—an old well-washed sheet, or cotton and dacron sheets are safe to use to pad the fold. We get the quilts out every so often to refold them so the folds don't get creased in. We do it once a year, but every couple of months would be better.

Also, quilts should be protected from humidity and from insects, dust, etc. It doesn't hurt to wrap them. An old sheet makes a good wrapper. Wrapping quilts in plastic is not such a good idea because the plastic can trap humidity.

Should the storage place also be free of humidity?
Yes. There's one quilt in our collection that somebody either had on a bed when it rained in the window or they had it in a trunk in the attic and the attic roof leaked or something like that. When that happens, you have moisture damage—and that's permanent damage. The dyes are not fast in the silks and late 19th-century fabrics.

How do you clean crazy quilts?
We don't. You really should leave them alone. They're not like cotton pieced quilts that you can wash. These are all silks and velvets. The colour would most certainly bleed if you put them in water. Many of the fabrics are very fragile, particularly the late 19th-century taffetas which were treated to make them crisp and rustling. That treatment makes them self-destruct after a while. Also, I wouldn't try to hang crazy quilts on display for long because the weight of the quilt itself might cause the fabric to tear.

If someone has a quilt in good condition that they'd like to hang for a short period, how do you recommend they do it?
One way is to sew a calico or cotton sleeve across the top of the quilt on the wrong side. Set it on by hand and then slip a dowel through the sleeve and hang it from the dowel.

Quilts in the TV series

THE FOUR ELEMENTS (	Radka Donnell
GUTCHEON SAMPLER (	Rhoda Cohen
SPREAD-OUT TOWN (	41 Fields Pond Road
TWO-TIERED TOWN	Weston
	MA 02193, USA
DIAMOND (	Nell Cogswell
	Box 99
	Carlisle
	MA 01741, USA
HILL TOWN (	Nancy Halpern

See 'Rhoda Cohen's Barns' by Nancy Halpern, *Qulter's Newsletter Magazine*, July August 1980

Bibliography

Bond, Dorothy. *Crazy Quilt Stitches*
34706 Row River Road, Cottage Grove, OR 97424, USA, 1981
(available by post)

Enthoven, Jacqueline. *The Stitches of Creative Embroidery*
Van Nostrand Reinhold Co, New York and Wokingham, USA, 1964

Haywood, Dixie. *The Contemporary Crazy Quilt Project Book*
Crown, 3536 Overholser Drive, Bethany, OK 73008, USA, 1977
(available by post)

Orlofsky, Patsy and Myron. *Quilts in America*
McGraw-Hill Book Co, New York, 1974 (regrettably out of print but may be obtainable through libraries)

Information on the care of quilts, pp331 41

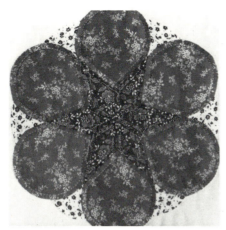

From Star Sampler—Ryker

Detail from Star of Bethlehem

Quilting is a fascinating pastime, but, like many interests, can be very time-consuming. If you like quilts but do not have the hours (or skills) necessary to make one, you can, of course, buy one. There are plenty of outlets both here and in the States for purchasing antique and contemporary quilts, and it is an activity that is increasing in popularity. A list of useful addresses has been included on p66 to enable you to track down sources.

Before buying a new quilt, there are some things you should be aware of. The first thing to consider is how you're going to use the quilt. If you're buying it to hang on a wall or to be part of a collection, you are really buying it as a piece of art and will be concerned primarily with the quilt's design.

If you're buying it for a bed, however, you also have to think about size and whether the materials used are going to wash and wear well. Use a blanket over the bed concerned to decide how large you want the quilt to be and take the measurements with you when you go to buy it.

Look closely at the material used in a quilt. Is it closely woven? If so, it will take a lot of wear and tear and be easy to wash. Also look at how well the quilt has been made. In a pieced quilt, for instance, take a look at the seams and make sure that they line up in straight lines and that the stitches are secure. Look also at any triangles or points on a quilt to see that they come to their complete point and are not cut off by seams. The binding, lattice strips and borders should all be straight.

In an appliquéd quilt, there are other things that you have to take into consideration. First, make sure that the appliqués are firmly sewn down and that the raw edges will stay folded under. Check any points. These will usually be the first area where raw edges will tend to come undone. Look at the stitching in appliqués. It shouldn't be easily noticed but should be done with small stitches right in the fold of the appliqué.

If it's a machine-appliquéd quilt, make sure that the satin stitches cover the raw edges of the appliqué completely and that they aren't going to come loose. And check to see that the appliqué lies flat.

Quilting stitches should be small and even. The quilting should look as if it's been done by one person even if it was done by a group. You shouldn't really be able to tell where one person started and another stopped. Also, you shouldn't be able to notice easily where the quilt was marked.

Take a look at how close the rows of stitching are. If the quilt has cotton wadding, the quilting lines should be no farther apart than about 2 inches. If it has polyester wadding or a cotton sheet or blanket for a filling, the quilting lines can be about 5 inches apart. The only way you can really tell what kind of wadding has been used in a quilt is to feel it. Cotton will feel very soft and very flat. Polyester will be a little bit fluffier and have a little more bounce to it.

The next thing to look at is the back of the quilt. Make sure that the type of material used for the back is also finely woven. And see where the quilt back has been pieced. It's good if it has been pieced along the centre or at equal distances in from the sides. You shouldn't be able to see any knots from the quilting either. They should all be hidden within the body of the quilt.

When you're buying an old quilt, there are additional things to consider. Carl Allen, an art history professor who has set up a quilt gallery in Ohio, USA, explains what he looks for when buying a quilt:

The most basic thing I look for is colour and design; secondly, craftsmanship. Being a quilt dealer, I also look at the desirability of the quilt. Certain colours sell better than others and thus demand higher prices. I look at how well it's put together, how many stitches per inch, how thin the quilt is, how even the edges are, how flat it lies.

Does the condition of the quilt have a great deal to do with its value?
It does except when the quilt is very rare or old. Then condition is not nearly as important as it would be on a quilt that's from around the turn of the century. There are more of those, so condition becomes important, because people know that they can find better quilts around.

When you have a quilt that needs small repairs such as an appliqué coming loose, can a person mend those small areas carefully without altering the value?
Whenever you restore something, the thing to remember is don't restore it so it cannot be put back in its original condition. And secondly, when you restore it, make sure that the colour and the tones are right and also that the fabric is from the same period as the quilt.

Sunshine Quilt auction

One interesting way of buying a quilt in the USA is by attending the quilt auctions organised in October in Ohio by the Mennonite religious organisation to raise money for a children's home there. Helen Dennis, coordinator of these auctions, explains how the auctions came about:

In 1949 when Sunshine Children's Home was started, there was a lot of support from the local Mennonite community in Ohio . . . Many of the Mennonite ladies had a history of traditional quilting and a history of helping people. So, combining these two interests, they came up with the quilt auction. We began it in 1973, and since that time it's really grown and developed.

It's interesting to sit down and talk to the quilt-makers and hear them tell stories of when they were little and their mothers would sit down and patiently show them how to make each stitch, and to make sure that they had consistency and that type of thing. And they are teaching their children today. So it looks like the tradition of quilting is going to continue on and on and on.

The majority of the quilts that we get donated for this event are made by Mennonite sewing circles throughout the country. We have had quilts donated from as far as Florida and Iowa as well as from all over the Midwest.

The Sunshine Quilt is very special to this event. The ladies' auxiliary is responsible for this quilt. It's a team process where one lady in the auxiliary will express an interest in the designing and we will sit and talk about her design, which is really important.

Judy Etchen, the designer of the 1980 Sunshine Quilt, describes her involvement in the project.

How did you arrive at the design for the quilt?
I started thinking about the designing of this quilt a year ago. I really wanted it to represent the Sunshine Home and the Sunshine logo, which is the big smiling sun. So I started with that in the middle on a piece of graph paper, and I expanded it from there. I tried to think of something that many women could work on at the same time. In our group we have women who are excellent at piecing quilts, and we have a couple of women who are very good at appliqué. I wanted something that many hands could work on.

So, somehow we arrived at the sampler quilt which has 20 sampler blocks all around the outside. Each block was pieced by a different woman. Someone else appliquéd the sun in the centre. When we had our first workshop after I had designed the quilt, I made up scale drawings of each of the blocks on a piece of graph paper. I made them exactly the size that each quilt block should be, and I coded where the colours should go because there were 10 different fabrics to work with.

The Sunshine Bazaar is held every year on the fourth Friday and Saturday in October at Southwyck Mall, Maumee, Ohio. The auction takes place on Saturday. Further information is available from Sunshine Children's Home, 7233 Maumee-Western Road, Maumee, Ohio 43537, USA

For more information on Mennonite quilt auctions, contact: Relief Sale Board, PO Box 243, Goshen, IN 46526, USA

1976 Sunshine Quilt illustrated in *Quilter's Newsletter Magazine*, October 1977, p9

Sunshine Quilt (Detail).

Some of the women said, 'I've never pieced anything before'. So we had a little instruction . . . And they did a really, really good job. Most were pieced by machine.

I tried to get a good sampling of pieced and appliquéd blocks that were very, very traditional. People who make quilts would know at a glance what they were. And I tried to get some that were more intricate than others to get a good sampling. And then, of course, there's the sun in the middle which ties the whole thing together. And that's really an excellent example of appliqué.

We wanted to get this quilt finished early because we had an idea to enter it in a national quilt show. So we started in January and had our first workshop. We gave everybody six weeks to complete the 20 blocks and get them back to me. In the meantime someone was also working on the sun in the centre and on the four suns in the corners of the quilt. Then we had another workshop where we got together and cut all the triangles for the borders and all the strips so that the entire quilt could all be put together. When all the pieces came back to me (20 finished blocks, the centre block and the four corner blocks), we started piecing the borders and constructing the whole quilt from the centre out.

How was the quilting done?

Our group numbers about 20 and not everybody is a quilter, so we put out a plea to everybody that knew anybody who liked to quilt. We put this quilt in the largest quilt frame that we could find and set it up in the basement of the Children's Home. The first day the ladies came at 9 o'clock in the morning, and the frame was filled all around. We must have had some 20 people quilting. And they quilted all day, every day, for a week. Different women came in each day. It took us a week and a day to quilt it.

The 1980 Sunshine Sampler, designed by Judy Etchen and made by the Sunshine Children's Home women's auxiliary, brought a final auction bid of $1000.

Contemporary quilt-makers are helping to advance quilt-making as an art form. This chapter looks at some of the philosophies and ideas of some American quilt-makers—Nancy Crow, Michael James, and Joyce Parr.

Nancy Crow

Nancy Crow is known for the way she uses stripes and plain colours in her work. She often designs a series of quilts, reworking the same designs in striking variations. One series is called 'Bittersweet'. This represents a series of stages in a relationship between two people, from a simple beginning, gradually growing in complexity of colour and design, to a dark period representing uncertainty and boredom, and finally emerging into a mature state.

Nancy began making quilts in 1975 and is now well established as a contemporary designer. Her advice to those who are beginning to design and make quilts of their own is to force yourself to set aside time to experiment, whatever your other commitments. 'I think it's absolutely important. And if you can't do that, if you come up with excuses . . . then that means you don't really have the drive to do it. So you had better re-examine your motives and maybe even forget it. Quilting is an extremely tedious process, other than the creative part. You just have to want to do it.'

Michael James

Michael James is a quilt-maker who is well known in America. Many of his quilts are made up of curved strips cut from a wide variety of fabrics and pieced together by hand or machine in subtle colour combinations, often arranged so that there is a movement from light to dark values. He has influenced many other quilters through his two books on quilt design and the workshops at which he teaches. (See p13 for his method of working out pieced block designs using various squares and triangles of cut paper.)

How did you get started in what traditionally is known as a woman's art?
My approach to quilt-making has come out of my painting background. When I was finishing my graduate thesis degree work, I was working with stains on canvas. I found that I was becoming much more interested in the texture of the fabric rather than paint. So as sort of a natural step–off to working with fabric itself (I had been attracted to traditional quilt design so the graphic quality of those images appealed to me), I decided to start putting pieces together. I was very much interested in traditional patterns. Copying traditional patterns is the way most people orient themselves to quilt-making. But after a few, which I considered a type of technical apprenticeship, I began making my own images and continued from there.

Do you think it's important to learn the craft?
It's as important for a quilt-maker to know the tradition in quilt-making as it is for a painter to know the painting tradition, for a dancer to know the dancing tradition, etc. With an understanding of what it's all based on, you can then create new images and new ideas and go forward, occasionally casting an eye back to see what you can learn and what you can re-interpret. In order for quilt-making to develop as an art form, you have to look forward; I think more so now than ever before. I think that one of the things that's helped keep quilt-making grounded in the past is the constant looking backward instead of looking forward. I think people are starting to realise that it's one art form that has untapped reservoirs that could provide centuries of visual enjoyment.

From Bittersweet Series—Crow

From Bittersweet Series—Crow

From the Nancy Crow collection

See: Michael James in *Lady's Circle Patchwork Quilts Magazine*, No 22, 'The World of Michael James,' pp32–34

Quintet—James

Suntreader No 3—James

So in 10 or 20 years will we see new styles of quilt-making?
I can't image what it will be like 10 or 20 years from now. But I'm sure that it will be totally unlike anything we know right now.

What would you say to someone who was interested in quilting but thought they lacked creativity?
If it's somebody just starting to get interested in traditional quilt-making, then the obvious thing is to take a basic beginning course which will concentrate on technique. I think it's really important to get the technique down first, the craft end of it. At that point, if the person is intent on creating his or her own images, it's probably good to take advanced design workshops either geared to quilt-makers or foundation colour and design courses in art colleges.

Joyce Parr

Gambier, Ohio, USA was the site of a contemporary quilt show in 1981 which featured the work of Nancy Crow, Michael James and six other quilt-makers. The exhibition was organised by Joyce Parr, a painter and quilt-maker:

How did you first get interested in quilting?
Well, it started as a process of being identified with women who stay at home and make things. I was a wife and mother who was staying at home for 12 years raising children. After having been an active part of the art world (I taught at college and showed my work), I stopped doing all that. I was isolated from that world, in fact. But more and more I identified with the women around me who lived on farms and did the same thing women have done for centuries. Quilting connected me with that in a way that painting never did.

What are some of the stories behind the quilts in the show?
One quilt by Wenda von Weise has rather a sad story actually. Wenda had some neighbours whose farm was sold and partitioned for a housing development. She took photographs of each stage of this process. She then made a series of quilts commemorating the old farm.

The quilts of Radka Donnell have an abstract expressionist look to them. They are the most contemporary looking of all the quilts in the show. Radka's thought a lot about her quilts. She says that the reason they are important to her is because they provide a place where she has her own space. She talks about how so many women have to follow their husbands or fathers around and can't choose the kind of house they want to live in. Most of the decisions in the family are made by their father or husband. And they find in quilting a place where they can make their own decisions. She says that in learning to make the decisions about placement of pieces and colours, she's gained a lot of confidence in her own ability to make decisions. She also says that it's very important to her that her quilts be used as quilts. Many quilts can be used only as wall hangings. It's important, she says, to be able to wrap yourself up in her quilts. The touching element is very important to her. She says that women don't get enough touching. They have to give so much touching to other people and they don't get enough of their own. She sees quilting as a very comforting kind of thing for that reason.

Quilt design

If you want to develop your eye for good quilt design, try to visit all the quilt shows and museums that you can. And when you see a quilt that you like, try to analyse what you like about it (and also what you don't like). You can learn a lot that way. You can also learn a lot, of course, by reading books on quilting and by taking quilting classes. The best books and teachers won't limit you to particular quilt patterns, but will, instead, stress the basics of quilt design so that you'll know enough then to either duplicate old quilt patterns if that is what you want or to create new ones of your own.

Judi Warren, a quilting teacher at the Toledo Museum of Art, made this observation about contemporary quilting: 'If we're going to make quilts in any form in the 1980s, we are duty bound to add to the heritage, not just keep repeating the same images. They were beautiful and wonderful, but we have our own images, and these should be added to that store of the design heritage. We take designs from the traditional, we shuffle them, we divide the square up in new ways. And then we begin to notice potential quilt designs everywhere. I think that's how it becomes current, vital and more than just a return to nostalgia.'

Contemporary quilts

The following quilts and artists appeared in the 'Contemporary Quilts' show at Colburn Gallery, Kenyon College, Gambier, Ohio:

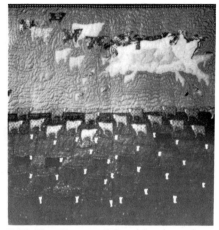

E B's New Pasture—Mangat

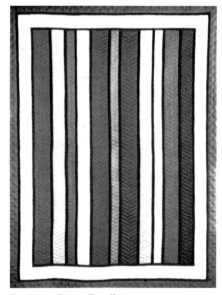

Spectrum Bars—Randles

NOVEMBER STUDY NO 1© NOVEMBER STUDY NO 2© NOVEMBER STUDY NO 3©	Nancy Crow Baltimore, Ohio
PRODIGAL DAUGHTER© WHOLENESS©	Radka Donnell Zurich, Switzerland
MAPLE LEAF WINDOW QUILTS (2)© HILLTOWN©	Nancy Halpern Natick, Massachusetts
SUNTREADER NO 3© QUINTET©	Michael James Somerset Village, Massachusetts (Courtesy of James Wallace Memphis, Tennessee)
E B 'S NEW PASTURE© GLITZ COWBOY©	Terrie Mangat Cincinnati, Ohio
THE GARDEN© THE FARM©	Joyce Parr Gambier, Ohio
SUNDOWN© SPECTRUM BARS©	Virginia Randles Athens, Ohio
FABRICATED LANDSCAPES© KNEALE FARM 1967–1977©	Wenda von Weise Cleveland Heights, Ohio

Quilts in the TV series

HILL TEMPLE©	Jan Myers 4234 Longfellow Avenue Minneapolis MN 55407, USA
AURORA AUSTRALIS©	Sue Hoyt 380 E Northwood Columbus OH 43201, USA
ATHENS FAREWELL© BITTERSWEET SERIES©	Nancy Crow 10545 Snyder Church Road Baltimore OH 43105, USA
DAWN NEBULA© QUARTET© SUNTREADER NO 3©	Michael James
PARISIAN CEREMONIAL MASK©	Francoise Barnes 162 E State Athens OH 45701, USA
UNTITLED©	Sue Hoyt
LAST DANCE OF FALL©	Nancy Erickson 3250 Pattee Canyon Road Missoula MT 59801, USA
SUMMER SKY©	Jan Myers
MIRAGE©	Maria McCormick-Snyder 9 Albany Street Cazenovia NY 13035, USA

Nancy Crow's work was featured in:
Fiberarts, September/October 1979 p81 and
Quilter's Newsletter Magazine, September
1980 p23; August 1980, p12. Also issues No
90 and No 114

Illustrated in: *Quilter's Newsletter Magazine*,
July/August 1981, p39

BIBLIOGRAPHY

Avery, Virginia. *The Big Book of Appliqué*
Bell & Hyman, 1978

Avery, Virginia. *Quilts to Wear*
Bell & Hyman, 1982

Betterton, Shiela. *Quilts and Coverlets from The American Museum in Britain*
The American Museum in Britain, Bath, 1978

Beyer, Jinny. *Patchwork Patterns*
Bell & Hyman, 1982

Beyer, Jinny. *The Quilter's Album of Blocks and Borders*
Bell & Hyman, 1982

Beyer, Jinny. *The Art and Technique of Creating Medallion Quilts*
Bell & Hyman, in press

Burbidge, Pauline. *Making Patchwork for Pleasure and Profit*
John Gifford, 1981

Cleaver, Joan. *Appliqué*
Search Press, 1978

Colby, Averil. *Patchwork/Quilting*
Batsford Craft Paperback Series, B T Batsford, 1983

da Conceição, Maria. *Finery*
Bell & Hyman, 1981

Echols, Margit. *Patterns for Patchwork Quilts*
Alphabooks, 1982

Fairfield, Helen. *Patchwork*
Octopus Books, 1980

Gutcheon, Beth. *The Perfect Patchwork Primer*
Penguin Books, 1974

Harding, Valerie. *Patchwork*
Search Press, 1978

Harding, Valeria. *Patchwork 2*
Search Press, 1983

Higgins, Muriel. *New Designs for Machine Patchwork*
B T Batsford, 1980

Ives, Suzy. *Patterns for Patchwork Quilts and Cushions*
B T Batsford, 1980

Johnstone, G. *Quilting*
Search Press, 1982

McKim, Ruby Short. *One Hundred and One Patchwork Patterns*
Constable & Co, 1967

McNeill, Moyra. *Quilting*
Octopus Books, 1980

Osler, Dorothy. *Machine Patchwork: Technique and Design*
B T Batsford, 1980

Richardson, Rosamond and Griffiths, Erica. *Discovering Patchwork*
BBC Publications, 1974

Rogers, Josephine. *The Seven-day Quilt*
Van Nostrand Reinhold, 1983

Short, Eirian. *Quilting: Technique, Design and Application*
B T Batsford, 1979

Walker, Michele, *Good Housekeeping: Quilting and Patchwork*
Ebury Press, 1983

USEFUL ADDRESSES

Whilst every care has been taken in compiling this list, we are aware that there may be inaccuracies and omissions and we apologise to suppliers who have not been included. It is always advisable to check opening times, etc, before making a special journey to any of the places mentioned. (Inclusion in this list does not imply recommendation and no liability can be accepted howsoever arising from any person, organisation or business listed below.)

Patchwork and quilting supplies

GENERAL

ENGLAND
Cambridgeshire
Lady Lodge Arts Centre, Orton Goldhay, Peterborough PE2 0JQ
Telephone 0733 237073
Books, fabrics, threads, templates, etc
Open: Monday–Friday 9–4 (also some evenings), weekends by arrangement

Devon
Strawberry Fayre, Chagford, Newton Abbot, Devon TQ13 8EN
Telephone 06473 3250
Wide range of English, European and American pure cotton fabrics and other quilt-making supplies. Mail order only, sae for catalogue

Dorset
Haven Handicrafts, 23 Church Street, Christchurch, Dorset
Telephone 0202 473935
Books, wadding, unbleached calico, templates, appliqué and quilting transfers, threads and hoops
Open: Monday–Saturday 9.30–5, also in summer Sunday 11–5 and evenings 8–10. Also mail order, sae for details

Magpie, 621 Wimborne Road, Winton, Bournemouth, Dorset BH9 2AR
Telephone 0202 524550
Fabrics, templates, hoops, wadding, England and American books, kits, etc
Open: Monday–Saturday 10–5 (closed Wednesday). Also mail order, large sae for details

The Patchwork Shoppe, The Old Mill, 13 Mill Lane, Wimborne, Dorset
Telephone 0202 881240
Books, hoops, templates, thread, fabrics etc
Open: Monday–Saturday 10–5. Also fabrics by post, sae for samples

Hampshire
Burdock Patch, 6 Barrow Hill, Goodworth Clatford, Andover,
Hampshire SP11 7RG
Telephone 0264 58118
Quilting and patchwork accessories, hoops, thread, templates, bindings, wadding and fine calico
Call by arrangement. Also mail order, sae for details

Green Hill Patchwork and Quilting, 27 Bell Street (above Ruskins), Romsey, Hampshire
Patchwork and quilting supplies
Open: Monday–Saturday 9.30–5.30

Hertfordshire
The Stables Studio, Dene Lane, Aston, Near Stevenage,
Hertfordshire SG2 7EP
Telephone 0438 88 271 & 308
Fabrics and border prints, wadding, templates, books, frames, threads, needles, etc. Also work in progress on view
Open: Tuesday–Sunday 11–4 (closed Monday). Large sae for current catalogue

London
Jan Davies, 9–11 Kensington High Street, London W8 6NP
Quilted cushion kits, exclusive designs
Send sae for details

John Lewis, Oxford Street, London W1 (also various provincial branches)
Telephone 01 629 7711
Large selection of fabrics; also wadding, thread, binding, kits, haberdashery

The Patchwork Dog and The Calico Cat, 21 Chalk Farm Road,
London NW1
Telephone 01 485 1239
*Fabric, threads, wadding, hoops and frames, English and American books, kits
and many aids for quilt-making. Also many quilts on view*
Open: Tuesday–Sunday 10–6 (closed Monday).
Also mail order, sae for catalogue

McCullock & Wallis Ltd, 25–26 Dering Street, London W1R 0BE
Telephone 01 629 0311
Wadding, fabric, thread, needles, etc
Open: Monday–Friday 9–5.15. Also mail order

Middlesex
Needles, 19 Church Street, Twickenham, Middlesex TW1 2QS
Telephone 01 892 9941
Templates, kits, rulers, books, threads, hoops, patchwork pieces
Open: Tuesday–Friday 10–6, Saturday 10–5

Norfolk
The Quiltery, Tacolneston, Norwich, Norfolk NR16 1DW
Telephone 050841 756
Templates, kits, packs and individual sheets of quilting patterns
Mail order only, sae for details and prices

Suffolk
The Needlecraft Shop, 4 Smallgate, Beccles, Suffolk NRQ34 9QQ
Telephone 0502 713543
Specialist wools, haberdashery and craft materials
Open:Monday–Saturday 9–5 (Wednesday 9–1)

Surrey
The Quilt Room, 37–39 High Street, Dorking, Surrey
Telephone 0306 889055
*Templates, polygrids, books, hoops, kits, cushion pads, thread, wadding, calico
and fabrics*
Open: Wednesday–Saturday 9–5.30 (closed Monday and Tuesday)

Yorkshire
Crimple Craft Ltd, South View, Beckwithshaw, Harrogate,
North Yorkshire HG3 1QR
Telephone 0423 69258
*Quilting needs, appliqué kits and the 'patch stamp' for marking out on fabric
or paper*
Mail order only, large sae for list

SCOTLAND
Aberdeen
Hobby House, 483 Great Western Road, Aberdeen
Telephone 0224 323678
Templates, wadding, threads, books, etc
Open: Monday–Saturday 9–5 (Wednesday 9–1)

Midlothian
Textile Workshop and Gallery, Gladstone's Land, Lawnmarket, Edinburgh
Telephone 031 225 4570
Templates, wadding, threads, books, etc
Open: Tuesday–Saturday 10–4

IRELAND
County Down
Design Workshops, 162 Portaferry Road, Newtownards, County Down
Telephone 024 774 422
Patchwork kits, quilting designs, templates, etc
Sae for stock list

Dublin
Stitch in Time, 3a Lower Georges Street, Dun Laoghaire, County Dublin
Telephone 01 809228
Books, templates, stencils, thread, 2 oz wadding, etc
Open: Monday and Wednesday 1–6, Saturday 10–6

Needle Craft, 27 Dawson Street, Dublin 2
Telephone 01 772493
Templates, kits, wadding, hoops, books, etc
Open: Monday–Friday 9–5.30, Saturday 9–1.
Mail order enquiries welcome (no catalogue)

FABRICS *(See also Patchwork and quilting supplies)*

ENGLAND
Berkshire
Village Fabrics, 44 Braywick Road, Maidenhead, Berkshire SL6 1DA
Telephone 0628 26749
Extensive range of VIP prints from America and fabric packs
Sae plus 50p for samples and details or sae for price list

Cambridgeshire
The Textile Studio, Free School Lane, Cambridge
Telephone 0223 313583
Fabrics from other countries, silks, etc
Personal shoppers only

Lancashire
J W Coates & Co Ltd, Croft Mill, Lowther Lane, Foulridge,
Colne, Lancashire
Telephone 0282 867979
Fabric sold by weight
Open: Monday–Saturday 10–4. Also mail order

A Garstang & Co Ltd, Dept F/QG, 213 Preston New Road,
Blackburn, Lancashire
Telephone 0254 59357
Fabrics by the metre
Open: Monday–Thursday 9–12.30, 1.30–5, Friday 9–12.30, 1.30–4.30 (closed Saturday). Also mail order, sae for patterns and details

Hartley's Fabrics, Bankfield Mill, Greenfield Road, Colne,
Lancashire BB8 9N1
Telephone 0282 868600
Open: Monday–Friday 9–5, Saturday 9–12. Also mail order, sae for details

Tritex Fabrics, 5 Fort Street, Accrington, Lancashire BB5 1QG
Telephone 0254 32015
Assorted fabrics
Mail order, sae plus 25p (refundable on first order) for details and samples

London
S Borovick, 16 Berwick Street, London W1
Telephone 01 437 2180
Large range of fabrics
Open: Monday–Friday 9–6, Saturday 9–1

The Fabric Studio, 10 Frith Street, 1st Floor, London W1
Telephone 01 434 2897
Open: Monday–Saturday 10–6

Pongees Ltd, 184–186 Old Street, London EC1
Telephone 01 253 0428
Importers of pure silk mainly in natural state for printing and dyeing, cutting charge for personal shoppers
Open: Monday–Friday 9–1, 2–5

George Weil & Sons Ltd, 63–65 Riding House Street, London W1P 7PP
Telephone 01 580 3763
Pure silk and cotton fabrics suitable for dyeing and printing, also 'Super Tinfix' paints for silk and wool
Open: Monday–Friday 9–5.30. Sae for price list and samples

Wiltshire
Cirel Greenwell, 2 The Old Court, Avoncliff, Bradford-on-Avon,
Wiltshire BA15 2HD
Patchwork fabrics from America including Jinny Beyer prints, also colouring sheets
Mail order only, sae for complete list of supplies

Yorkshire
Whaleys (Bradford) Ltd, Harris Court Mills, Great Horton Road, Bradford,
West Yorkshire BD7 4EQ
Telephone 0274 576718
Assorted fabrics
Mail order only, sae for price list

SCOTLAND
Midlothian
The Cloth Shop, 24 Craighall Road, Edinburgh 6
Telephone 031 552 8818
Fabrics and haberdashery
Open: Tuesday–Saturday 9.30–4 (till 8 pm Thursday)

COLOURING SHEETS

ENGLAND
Bedfordshire
Jean Denton, 25 Huntingdon Road, Kempston, Bedford
Hexagon design paper, packs of 5 sheets
Mail order only, sae for details

Wiltshire
Cirel Greenwell *(see under Fabrics)*
Colouring sheets: 4, 5 and 9 patch, isometric and log cabin
Mail order only, sae for complete list of supplies

TEMPLATES *(see also Patchwork and quilting supplies)*

ENGLAND
Hampshire
Patchwork Papers, 14 Dundonald Close, Hayling Island,
Hampshire PO11 9DX
Telephone 07016 66272
1½ inch hexagon plus compatible diamonds, half hexagons and triangles.
2 inch diamond plus half and quarter diamonds. 3 inch clamsell plus half shells
Mail order only, sae for details

London
Colers Patchplates, Sheilagh Jewers, 10 Barley Mow Passage, Chiswick,
London W4 4PH
Telephone 01 994 6477
Metal templates in ten shapes and a variety of sizes
Sae for details

QUILTING PATTERNS *(see also Patchwork and quilting supplies)*

ENGLAND
Durham
Durham County Federation of Women's Institutes, 51–52 Cross Gate,
Durham DH1 4PY
Telephone 0385 42041
North Country quilting patterns and booklet
Sae for details and prices

Norfolk
The Quiltery *(see under Patchwork and quilting supplies)*
Sheets and packs of quilting patterns
Mail order only, sae for details and prices

Wiltshire
CoSIRA, 141 Castle Street, Salisbury, Wiltshire SP1 3TP
Telephone 0722 6255
Drawings of traditional quilting patterns and quilting frame plans.
Also publishers of Craft Workshops in the English Countryside
Sae for prices and details

QUILTING FRAMES *(see also Patchwork and quilting supplies)*

ENGLAND
Hampshire
Abbotsdene Crafts, 76 Roman Road, Basingstoke, Hampshire RG23 8HB
Telephone 0256 25621
Quilting frame and stretching frame
Sae for details

Surrey
K & M Woodcraft, Tollers Design Centre for Arts and Crafts, Tollers Farm,
Drive Road, Old Coulsdon, Surrey
Telephone 07375 57673
Quilting frames and needlework boxes etc, ready-made and made to order
Sae for full details and prices

HAND QUILTING

ENGLAND
Devon
Lorna Jenkin, Bridle Cottage, Shobrooke, Crediton, Devon
Your patchwork quilted by craftswomen
Sae for details

COMMERCIAL QUILTING

ENGLAND
London Progressive Quilting Co Ltd, 221–225 West Ferry Road,
London E14
Telephone 01 987 4277
Your own fabric machine-quilted (metre width)
Sae for details

DYES

ENGLAND
London
London Textile Workshop, 65 Rosebery Road, London N10
Telephone 01 883 4190
Dyeing equipment, top quality dyes and chemicals for craftworkers available in
small quantities
Callers by appointment only. Mail order, sae for list and further details

LABELS

ENGLAND
West Midlands
J & J Cash Ltd, Designer Labels CR1, Kingfield Road, Coventry,
West Midlands CV1 4DU
Personalised woven labels for textile crafts
Sae for details

WALES
Gwynedd
Mary Ellen Designs, Dept CM1, Pen-y-Bryn, Trefriw, Gwynedd LL27 0JU
Wash-fast labels
Sae for samples and details

SCOTLAND
Berwickshire
Diverse Marketing (C), Westruther G, Gordon, Berwickshire TD3 6NE
Printed fabric labels, also the 'Printy' rubber stamp
Send stamp for catalogue and samples

BOOKS AND MAGAZINES *(see also Patchwork and quilting supplies and Bibliography)*

ENGLAND
Buckinghamshire
Craft Publications, 104 Salford Road, Aspley Guise, Milton Keynes,
Buckinghamshire MK17 8HZ
Telephone 0908 582743
American quilt and patchwork magazines: Quilt, Quilters Newsletter
Magazine, Fiberarts, *etc. Also books and patterns*
Sae for subscription details

Dorset
Sacketts, 36a Salisbury Street, Blandford, Dorset
Telephone 0258 53654
Second-hand and nearly new craft books. Also search service to find particular
titles and will buy good quality craft books
Sae for latest selected list

Gloucestershire
Roberts Bookshop, 23 Gloucester Street, Stroud, Gloucestershire GL5 1QG
Telephone 04536 79431
Specialise in craft books
Sae for list

London
Bayswater Books, 112a Westbourne Grove, London W2 5RU
Telephone 01 229 1432
Textile craft books and periodicals
Open: Monday–Saturday 10–5

Norfolk
Jenifer Frost, Hill House, Gresham, Norwich NR11 8RB
Second-hand books on needlework, embroidery, etc
Sae for list

Suffolk
Faith Legg, The Guildhall Bookroom, Church Street, Eye, Suffolk IP23 7BD
Telephone 0379 870 193
Second-hand books specialising in needlework
Open: Friday and Saturday or by arrangement

ANTIQUE QUILTS

ENGLAND
London
Christie's Auctions, Christie's South Kensington, 85 Old Brompton Road,
London SW7 3JS
Telephone 01 581 2231
Quilt sales held occasionally
Sae for list of forthcoming sales

The Patchwork Dog and The Calico Cat
(see under Patchwork and quilting supplies)
Antique and contemporary quilts from various countries

CARING FOR QUILTS

ENGLAND
London
The White Fleece, 16–17 Glendower Place, London SW7
Telephone 01 584 1246
Specialist dry cleaners
Send sae with any enquiries

Surrey
The Textile Conservation Centre, Apartment 22, Hampton Court Palace,
East Molesey, Surrey KT8 9AU
Address all enquiries to The Principal and enclose an sae

Courses

It is always worth enquiring from your Local Education Authority whether
they run embroidery or patchwork evening classes which may include some
quilt work. They often also have residential colleges for adults which may
feature short courses on quilting or patchwork. As well as the private courses
listed here, the Quilters' Guild runs some classes, as does the Embroiderers'
Guild. (Inclusion in this list does not imply recommendation.)

ENGLAND
Berkshire
Studio 23, Steward House, 23 Frances Road, Windsor, Berkshire
Telephone 07535 69566
Half and one-day courses several times a year
Sae for details

Cambridgeshire
Lady Lodge Arts Centre, Orton Goldhay, Peterborough PE2 0JQ
Telephone 0733 237073
Day and evening courses and specialist workshops in patchwork and quilting
for adults and children
Sae for details

Cheshire
Styal Workshop, Quarry Bank Mill, Styal, Cheshire SK9 4LA
Telephone 0625 527 468
Wide range of textile courses
Sae for details

Dorset
The Patchwork Shoppe, The Old Mill, 13 Mill Lane, Wimborne, Dorset
Telephone 0202 881240
Workshops
Sae for details

Hampshire
Green Hill Patchwork and Quilting, 27 Bell Street (above Ruskins),
Romsey, Hampshire
Advice and classes
Sae for details

The Indigo Workshops, 4 Lenten Street, Alton, Hampshire GU34 1HD
Telephone 0420 87285 & 85883
Tuition offered for 10-week terms and weekend courses in textiles
Sae for details

Hertfordshire
The Stables Studio, Dene Lane, Aston, Near Stevenage,
Hertfordshire SG2 7EP
Telephone 043888 271 & 308
One-day courses on a variety of patchwork techniques from March to October
Sae for details

Lancashire
Gawthrope Hall, Padiham, Near Burnley, Lancashire BB12 8AU
Telephone 0282 78511
Facilities for personal study by arrangement; also textile courses
Sae for details

London
The Patchwork Dog and The Calico Cat, 21 Chalk Farm Road,
London NW1
Telephone 01 485 1239
Courses on all aspects of patchwork and quilting
Sae for details

Stitch Design, 120 Cannon Workshops, West India Dock, Isle of Dogs,
London E14
*Needlecraft courses in a wide variety of subjects. Family days in the
school holidays*
Sae for details

Shropshire
Westhope College, Craven Arms, Seifton, Shropshire
Telephone 058 473 293
*Patchwork courses available for residential and non-residential students.
Children accepted; facilities also for disabled*
Sae for details

Surrey
Tollers Design Centre for Arts and Crafts, Tollers Farm, Drive Road,
Old Coulsdon, Surrey
Telephone 07375 57673
Sae for details

Sussex
Residential Adult Education College, The Old Rectory, Fittleworth,
Pulborough, Sussex RH20 1HU
Telephone 079 882 306
*Residential and non-residential courses on a wide range of subjects including
patchwork. Children accepted*
Sae for details

West Midlands
Midlands Art Centre, Cannon Hill Park, Birmingham B12 9QH
Telephone 021 440 4221
Textile courses
Sae to Head of Textiles for further details

SCOTLAND
Midlothian
Textile Workshop and Gallery, Gladstone's Land, Lawnmarket, Edinburgh
Telephone 031 225 4570
Various textile courses
Sae for details

IRELAND
Dublin
Stitch in Time, 3a Lower Georges Street, Dun Laoghaire, County Dublin
Telephone 01 809228
Saturday afternoon workshops (2–5.30) on embroidery, tapestry and stained
glass patchwork
Sae for further details

Museums and houses where quilts may be seen

Quilts are not normally on display but are kept in the museum's reference
collection for research and study purposes; they may therefore only be
available at the discretion of the Curator. Whilst every care has been taken in
compiling this list, it is always advisable to check dates and times.

ENGLAND
Avon
The American Museum in Britain, Claverton Manor, Bath, Avon BA2 7BD
Telephone 0225 60503 (Education Dept: 63538)
Large collection and display of American quilts.
Talks to parties can be arranged on application to the Secretary
Open: 26 March–30 October, daily 2–5 (closed Monday)

City of Bristol Museum and Art Gallery, Queen's Road, Bristol 8, Avon
Telephone 0272 299771
Quilts; textiles in store may be viewed by appointment only
Open: Monday–Saturday 10–5

Cumbria
Abbot Hall Museum of Lakeland Life and Industry, Abbot Hall,
Kendal, Cumbria
Telephone 0539 22464
Patchwork and other textiles. Room settings include some quilts
Write for appointment to view items in store
Open: Weekdays 10.30–5, weekends 2–5 (closed for two weeks over
Christmas–New Year, also Good Friday)

Levens Hall, Kendal, Cumbria LA8 0PB
Telephone 0448 60321
*The earliest English patchwork quilt (*circa *1708) and other fine needlework*
Contact the Proprietor
Open: Easter Sunday–29 September, Tuesday, Wednesday, Thursday, Sunday
and Bank Holiday Monday 11–5

Devon
Royal Albert Memorial Museum and Art Gallery, Queen Street,
Exeter, Devon
Telephone 0392 56724
Thirteen patchwork items and seventeen quilted garments.
Write or telephone the Curator to arrange appointment to view
Open: Tuesday–Saturday 10–5.15

Durham
North of England Open Air Museum, Beamish, Stanley, County Durham
Telephone 0207 31811
One of the finest collections of quilts in Britain, some on view in the cottages and
Beamish Hall, others by arrangement with the Keeper of Social History
Open: April–September, daily 10–6. October–March, daily 10–5 (closed
Monday)

The Bowes Museum, Barnard Castle, County Durham
Telephone 0833 37139
Another fine collection of quilts, a few on display, others can be viewed by
arrangement with the Curator
Open: May–September, Monday–Saturday 10–5.30, Sunday 2–5. October,
March, April 10–5. November–February 10–4, Sunday 2–4

Gloucestershire

Cheltenham Art Gallery and Museum, Clarence Street, Cheltenham, Gloucestershire
Telephone 0242 37431
Small collection of interesting quilts in good condition kept in reserve collection
To view, write (giving plenty of notice) to Assistant Keeper of Applied Arts
Open: Monday–Saturday 10–5.30 (closed Sunday and Bank Holidays)

Herefordshire

Hereford City Museum and Art Gallery, Broad Street, Hereford
Telephone 0432 268121, extension 207
Hereford City Museums have a number of quilts which may be viewed by appointment with the Curator
Open: Tuesday, Wednesday and Friday 10–6, Thursday and Saturday 10–5 (closed at 4 on Saturday in Winter); closed Monday

Isle of Man

The Manx Museum, Douglas
Telephone 0624 5522
About 30 patchwork bedcovers.
Appointments to view should be made with the Curator
Open: Monday–Saturday 10–5 (closed Sunday)

Lancashire

Gawthorpe Hall, Padiham, Near Burnley, Lancashire BB12 8UA
Telephone 0282 78511
The Rachel Kay-Shuttleworth collection of embroidery, lace and costume, including 60 quilts and patchworks in a variety of techniques dating from the 18th century to the present day.
Available for personal study by arrangement with the Curator
Open: Mid March–end October, Wednesday, Saturday, Sunday and Bank Holiday Monday (also Tuesday in July and August) 2–6. November–end December, Tuesday, Wednesday, Saturday and Sunday 2–5

London

Gunnersbury Park Museum, Gunnersbury Park, London W3 8LQ
Telephone 01 992 1612
Some patchwork and other textiles including costume
Open: March–October, Monday–Friday 1–5, Saturday, Sunday and Bank Holidays 2–6, November–February, Monday–Friday 1–4, Saturday, Sunday and Bank Holidays 2–4

Victoria and Albert Museum, Cromwell Road, South Kensington, London SW7 2RL
Telephone 01 589 6371
Small collection of quilts on general view.
Arrangements should be made well in advance with the Keeper, Department of Textiles, for small groups to view items in store
Open: Monday–Thursday and Saturday 10–5.50 (closed Friday), Sunday 2.30–5.50

Norfolk

Strangers' Hall, Charing Cross, Norwich, Norfolk NR2 4AL
Telephone 0603 611277, extension 275
Approximately 50 quilts in the collection. View by arrangement with the Curator
Open: Monday–Saturday 10–5

Northumberland

Cragside House and Country Park, Rothbury, Morpeth, Northumberland NE65 7PX
Telephone 0669 20333
Victorian quilts on some of the beds
Open: April–end September, daily (closed Monday, except Bank Holiday Monday) 1–6. October, Wednesday, Saturday and Sunday 2–5

Sussex

Glynde Place, Glynde, Near Lewes, East Sussex
Eighteen embroidered and quilted bed covers in excellent condition
Open: Mid May–mid October, Wednesday and Thursday 2.15–5.30

Worthing Museum and Art Gallery, Chapel Road, Worthing, West Sussex
Telephone 0903 39999, extension 121
About 40 quilts.
For appointment to view give a few days' notice to Assistant Curator of Costume
Open: Monday–Saturday 10–6 (October–March 10–5)

Tyne & Wear
Shipley Art Gallery, Prince Consort Road South, Gateshead,
Tyne & Wear NE4 4JB
Telephone 0632 771495
One traditional quilt on display. Information on North Country quilts and
quilters by arrangement with the Curator
Open: Monday–Saturday 10–5.30, Sunday 2–5, Bank Holidays 10–5.30

Yorkshire
The Castle Museum, Tower Street, York Y01 1RY
Telephone 0904 53611
Quilt on view in 'moorland cottage'. Collection of quilts not on general display.
Requests for private views and seminars should be made in writing to the Keeper
of Textiles, specifying arrangements required
Open: April–September, Monday–Saturday 9.30–6.30, Sunday 10–6.30.
October–March, Monday–Saturday 9.30–4.30, Sunday 10–4.30

WALES
South Glamorgan
Welsh Folk Museum, St Fagans, Cardiff CF5 6XB
Telephone 0222 569441
Collection not normally on view. Some items may be viewed and talks available
on request to Head of Department, Domestic and Corporate Life
Open: Monday–Saturday 10–5, Sunday 2.30–5

SCOTLAND
Edinburgh
Royal Scottish Museum, Chambers Street, Edinburgh EH1 1JF
Telephone 031 225 7534
Material in store may be viewed by appointment
Open: Monday–Saturday 10–5, Sunday 2–5

NORTHERN IRELAND
Armagh
Armagh County Museum, The Mall East, County Armagh
Telephone 0861 523070
Quilts; the reserve collection may be viewed by appointment
Open: Monday–Saturday 10–1, 2–5 (closed certain Bank Holidays)

Down
Ulster Folk and Transport Museum, Cultra Manor, Holywood,
County Down BT18 0 EU
Telephone 023 17 5411
Large collection of quilts and coverlets. Some on view in 'Open Air' section.
Reserve collection can be viewed by arrangement with Keeper, Department
of Textiles
Open: Summer months, Monday–Saturday 11–6, Sunday 2–6

Guilds and societies

THE QUILTERS' GUILD

The Quilters' Guild was founded in August 1979 by a group who felt that their craft might find wider appeal throughout Britain. It is a national organisation for quilt-makers and quilt-lovers which aims to promote, through education in the widest sense, a greater understanding of the art, techniques and heritage of patchwork, appliqué and quilting. It also aims to encourage and maintain the highest standards of workmanship and design in both traditional and contemporary work. By bringing quilt-makers together and keeping them informed, the Guild hopes to foster a climate of cooperation amongst quilt-makers in this country and with those abroad.

To these ends, The Quilters' Guild publishes a quarterly newsletter which contains information on all Guild activities, news from regional groups and a diary section listing forthcoming exhibitions and classes; there are also articles, sewing tips, patterns and reviews. The Guild organises exhibitions, lectures, conferences, workshops and visits to museums with collections of interest to quilt-makers. An increasing number of specialist books, slides, quilts and patterns are available to members for study purposes. Also a wide network of regional representatives enables the Guild to maintain contact with groups and individuals.

Plans for the future include more work with teachers and young quilters, and researching and recording our quilt-making heritage. Membership of The Quilters' Guild is open to anyone who enjoys doing patchwork, appliqué or quilting or has a specialist interest in quilts. For further information about the Guild or regional groups, contact:

Margaret Petit (Secretary, The Quilters' Guild), 56 Wilcot Road, Pewsey, Wiltshire SN9 5EL
Telephone 067 26 3230

To ensure an answer please enclose a stamped, addressed envelope.

PATCHWORK GUILD, NORTHERN IRELAND

The Patchwork Guild was founded in March 1979. Meetings are held at the Ulster Folk Museum from September to June on the first Saturday in each month. The Guild publishes a quarterly newsletter and organises exhibitions, workshops, guest speakers and demonstrations. Membership is mainly from Northern Ireland with a few from Eire. For further information send a stamped, addressed envelope to:

Dr Joan Donaldson, 19 Glencraig Park, Craigavad, County Down, Northern Ireland

IRISH PATCHWORK SOCIETY, IRISH REPUBLIC

The Irish Patchwork Society was founded in June 1981. The Society publishes a quarterly newsletter and also organises exhibitions, lectures and workshops, and encourages the forming of local groups. Membership is mainly from the Republic but there are a few members from England, America and even Japan. For information about the Irish Patchwork Society, contact:

Ann McDermott (The Information Officer), 8 Raheen Green, off Blessington Road, Tallaght, County Dublin, Irish Republic
Telephone 01 513373

Please enclose a stamped, addressed envelope.

THE EMBROIDERS' GUILD

This long-established guild, based at Hampton Court Palace, has over 100 branches in the UK and runs classes, dayschools and exhibitions which often include quilting. Their quarterly magazine, *Embroidery*, frequently has articles on quilting and the guild has an extensive collection of historical needlework to which members have access. Membership is open to all who are interested in the subject; for more information write to:

The Secretary, The Embroiderers' Guild, Apartment 41a, Hampton Court Palace, East Molesey, Surrey KT8 9AU
Telephone 01 943 1229

INDEX